D0093703

Voices in the Air

To Manage

She writes to me—
    I can't sleep because I'm seventeen
Sometimes I lie awake thinking
    I didn't even clean my room yet
And soon I will be twenty-five
    And a failure
And when I am fifty—oh!
I write her back
    Slowly   slow
Clean one drawer
    Arrange words on a page
Let them find one another
    Find you
Trust they might know something
    You aren't living   the whole thing
       At once

That's what a minute   said to an hour
Without me   you are nothing

Aurora Borealis
(Fairbanks, Alaska)

The light was speaking to me
stretching out its long gleaming fingers
pointing down
maybe it could hear my shout
shimmering green parentheses
put me in my place
my place was low
every earthbound element
Alaska Gas
Sam's Sourdough Café
lifting into radiance

snow felt less cold
tiny human leaping
under green swoops
rippled fringes
staggering swish
middle of night
by myself
not by myself
came so close

NAOMI SHIHAB NYE

Voices in the Air

POEMS FOR LISTENERS

GREENWILLOW BOOKS

An Imprint of HarperCollinsPublishers

The text of this book is set in 12-point Bembo.

Book design by Paul Zakris

Library of Congress Cataloging-in-Publication Data

Names: Nye, Naomi Shihab, author.
Title: Voices in the air : poems for listeners / by Naomi Shihab Nye.
Description: New York, N.Y. : Greenwillow Books, 2018. |
Includes bibliographical references and indexes. |
Summary: "Ninety-five poems pay tribute to essential voices past and present that have the power to provoke us, lead us, and give us hope"—Provided by publisher.
Identifiers: LCCN 2017046142 | ISBN 9780062691842 (hardcover)
Subjects: LCSH: Inspiration—Juvenile poetry. |
Hope—Juvenile poetry.
Classification: LCC PS3564.Y44 A6 2018 | DDC 811/.54—dc23
LC record available at https://lccn.loc.gov/2017046142

18 19 20 21 22 PC/LSCH 10 9 8 7 6 5 4 3 2 1
First Edition

GREENWILLOW BOOKS

For Connor James Nye and Virginia Duncan

In memory, Paula Merwin, Paul Rode, Bill Hanson,
Thomas Lux, James Tolan, Catherine Kasper, Brother Tony Hearn

Contents

SECTION II: VOICES IN THE AIR

SECTION III: MORE WORLDS

Introduction

Poet Galway Kinnell said, "To me, poetry is someone standing up, so to speak, and saying, with as little concealment as possible, what it is for him or her to be on earth at this moment."

Someone—Abraham Lincoln?—once remarked that all the voices ever cast out into the air are still floating around in the far ethers—somehow, somewhere—and if we only knew how to listen well enough, we could hear them even now.

Voices as guides, lines and stanzas as rooms, sometimes a single word the furniture on which to sit . . . each day we could open the door, and enter, and be found. These days I wonder—was life always strange—just strange in different ways? Does speaking some of the strangeness help us survive it, even if we can't solve or change it?

Where is my map—where are we, please? Can voices that entered into our thoughts when we were little help us make amends with the strange time we're in?

William Stafford, great twentieth-century American poet and teacher, tireless encourager of dialogue and nonviolence, is still speaking in the slant shadows falling across the path. If we only knew how to listen better, he said, even the grasses by the roadsides could help us live our lives. They're flexible, for one. What might he say about our current moments in history? Would he be surprised by the divisive rhetoric, mysterious backsliding? Or not surprised at all?

When I see a highway sign, "No Right Turn onto Whirlwind Drive"—Stafford comes to mind. He carried a decisive calm.

Peter Matthiessen, the only American writer ever to win the National Book Award in both fiction and nonfiction, is still standing out on his Long Island beach, staring at the sky, asking us, *Did you see that? Flying over just now? Did you catch the span of the wings, the rosy tip of the head?*

Might we pause on our way to everywhere we are rushing off to and hear something in the air, old or new, that would make sense?

~

Not so long ago we were never checking anything in our hands, scrolling down, pecking with a finger, obsessively tuning in. My entire childhood did not involve a single deletion. These are relatively new acts on earth.

In those archaic but still vivid days, there might be a meandering walk into trees, an all-day bike ride, a backyard picnic, a gaze into a stream, a plunge into a sunset, a conversation with pines, a dig in the dirt, to find our messages. When we got home, there was nothing to check or catch up on—no one speaking to us in our absence.

Recently, when I had the honor of visiting Yokohama International School in Japan to conduct poetry workshops, student Juna Hewitt taught me an important word— *Yutori*—"life-space." She listed various interpretations for its meaning—arriving early, so you don't have to rush. Giving yourself room to make a mistake. Starting a diet, but not beating yourself up if you eat a cookie after you started it. Giving yourself the possibility of succeeding. (Several boys in another class defined the word as when the cord for your phone is long enough to reach the wall socket.) Juna said she felt that reading and writing poetry gives us more *yutori*—a place to stand back to contemplate what we are living and experiencing. More spaciousness in being, more room in which to listen.

I love this. It was the best word I learned all year.

Not that sense of being nibbled up—as if message minnows surround us at all moments, nipping, nipping at our edges.

Perhaps we have more voices in the air now—on TV, in our phones and computers and little saved videos—but are we able to hear them as well? Are these the voices we really need? Is our listening life-space deep enough? Can we tell ourselves when we need to walk away from chatter, turn it off entirely for half a day, or a full day, or a whole weekend, ease into a realm of something slower, but more tangible?

Can we go outside and listen?

In 1927 Freya Stark, an English writer born in Paris in 1893, who would become known for her astonishing travels through even the most remote parts of the Middle East, paused for a picnic near some Roman ruins outside Damascus. She wrote, "We ate our food with little clouds of Roman sand blown off the hewn stones and thought of the fragility of things." Near Baghdad she wrote, ". . . in the morning all is peace, and all went out to pasture. The camels, looking as if they felt that their walk is a religious ceremony, went further afield; they are comparatively independent, needing to drink only once in four days; the sheep and goats stayed nearer. And when they had all gone, and melted invisibly into the desert face, the empty luminous peace again descended, lying round us in light and air and silence for the rest of the day."

Freya Stark's light and air and silence feel palpable in her paragraphs. Her respect for people unlike herself, her fascination with worlds very different from the European ones she had grown up in—yet fully recognizable in their humanity and hope—heartens me when my own time feels too odd to bear. Her curious voice traveling through the air is more comforting than people currently claiming power, demanding recognition, trying to make others feel as if they don't belong. Literature gives us a home in bigger time.

But how do we find our ways home? Continually, regularly? With so much vying for our attention, how do we listen better? Reminding ourselves of what we love feels helpful. Walking outside—it's as quiet as it ever was. The birds still communicate without any help from us. In that deep quietude, doesn't the air, and the memory, feel more full of voices? If we slow down and intentionally practice listening, calming our own clatter, maybe we hear those voices better. They live on in us. Take a break from multitasking. Although many of us are no longer sitting on rocks in deserts watching camels, sheep, and goats heading out to pasture, we could sit. In a porch swing? On the front steps? In a library or coffee shop? On a park bench? Quiet inspiration may be as necessary as food, water, and shelter. Try giving yourself regular times a day for reading and thinking—even if just for a minute or two. Mindfulness, many agree, is profoundly encouraged by regular practice. A different sort of calm begins feeling like the true atmosphere behind everything else. If you're an "I read before I go to sleep" sort of person, why not add a little more I-just-got-home-from-school-or-work reading? In the modern world, we deserve to wind down. Or perhaps some morning reading, to launch yourself? How long does it take to read a poem? Slowing to a more gracious pacing—trying not to hurry or feel overwhelmed—inch by inch—one thought at a time—can be a deeply helpful mantra. It's a gift we give our own minds.

The melancholy, brilliant singer-songwriter Townes Van Zandt died suddenly on New Year's Day 1997. His many fans were stunned and saddened. That was the first day our son showed me I could "enter the world wide web" to read obituaries and stories about Townes rising suddenly from all over the world—Nashville, London, Berlin. Incredible! How had this happened? Everything was now—available? The searching process felt exotic, haunting, and comforting—fans around the world, grieving for Townes together. His song lines kept rising in my mind for months afterward. "If I needed you, would you come to me?"

I think they all would. All the voices we ever loved or respected in our lives would come. And they would try to help us.

—*Naomi Shihab Nye*
San Antonio, Texas

MESSAGES

Broken pencil

Broken pen

Maybe today

I'll write my best poem

I almost felt
more than I had
been waiting for
what possible tellings
purple   purple   purple

You saw   nothing
knew   nothing
    before   now

Now   what
do   you   know?

Propriety

How dare they they they
say say say
anything we can or cannot do with our own
red and blue
We are voting for ourselves
unbound by convention
your convention
I refuse to go to the convention
too many people
we will kiss in the hotel hallway
if we please
you and me
New York City on the last day of an old year
in future anytime
EXIT door to hotel stairway appears
feel a sizzle
swizzle stick of memory spinning me
through so much dullness
red and blue

Big Bend National Park
Says No to All Walls

Big Bend has been here, been here.
    Shouldn't it have a say?
Call the mountains a wall if you must,
    (the river has never been a wall),
leavened air soaking equally into all,
    could this be the home
we ache for? Silent light bathing cliff faces,
    dunes altering
in darkness, stones speaking low to one another,
    border secrets,
notes so rooted you may never be lonely
    the same ways again.
Big bend in thinking—why did you dream
    you needed so much?
Water, one small pack. Once I lay on my back
    on a concrete table
the whole day and read a book.
    A whole book and it was long.
The day I continue to feast on.
Stones sifting a gospel of patience and dust,

no one exalted beyond a perfect parched cliff,

no one waiting for anything you do or don't do.

Santa Elena, South Rim, once a woman here knew

what everything was named for. Hallie Stillwell,

brimming with stories, her hat still snaps in the wind.

You will not find a prime minister in Big Bend,

a president or even a candidate, beyond the lion,

the javelina, the eagle lighting on its nest.

Time's Low Note

When the giant moon
rises over the river,
the cat stretches,
presses himself to the window,
croons.
He needs to go outside
into dark grass
to feel the mystery
combing his fur.

The wind never says
    Call me back,
        I'll be waiting for your call.
All we know about wind's address is
somewhere else.

A peony has been trying   to get through to you
    When's the last time   you really looked at one?
    Billowing pinkish whitish petals   lushly layered
      Might be the prime object of the universe

    Peonies   in a house

          profoundly uplift   the house
never say no   to peonies
Some days   reviewing everything
          from brain's balcony
                   filigree of thinking   a calm comes in
     you can't fix the whole street   change the city
or the world
               but clearing bits of rubbish possible

                              moving one stone

Bully

One boy in our grade school was considered
    a bully—
muttering rude insults under his breath,
tripping girls as they walked to their desks.
He bothered everyone equally, shook his shaggy
blond hair when teachers called his name.
My mom, hearing the tales, decided he was lonely
(no one ever played with him—in those days

        bullies weren't popular)
and committed me to attending
a children's Christmas party with him
in the basement of a Methodist church.
Somehow she arranged this plan with his mother
as they waited for us by the schoolyard.
Impressive he had a mother who waited—
he seemed like a person who sprang from a forest,
growling.
My parents argued about the Christmas party
every night before it happened.
Daddy said Mom was "sacrificing me to her idealism."
He kept calling it my "first date."

I was only interested in what people did
in basements of churches
and what I would wear and would there be cake.
Since we ate no sugar at our house (idealism),
I dreamed of meeting sweets everywhere else.
The night of the party, Bully wore a suit
and striped tie. He didn't growl.
It was his church, but he didn't seem to know
anyone.
I stood in my puffed pink icing of a ruffled dress
by the cake table and watched him.
He skulked around
while the choir sang Christmas songs,
looked embarrassed when Santa appeared.
I talked to him any time he came near.
Would you like some cake? I don't recall him
bothering me again at school for the rest of our years.

Invocation

She wanted to be a window wherever she walked.

Light of beauty might shine through,

but also she felt the small animal cry—"trapped."

Someone else directing what to do.

Maybe trucks roaring past in the rain

held a clue in the spin of their wheels.

We could never see what they carried,

wasn't that strange? All those trucks

on the highways of the world, packed with secrets.

Maybe the smallest thistle volunteering

near the fence, growing unnoticed,

or the person we'd never meet,

who never heard of us either,

walking in twilight on the beach at Sharjah,

dipping burgundy cloth into a soaking vat at

   Mumbai,

crying for what was gone from Aleppo,

maybe they knew the best ways to survive.

To be alive was a wall, as often as a door.

But to live like a movable hinge . . .

Bamboo Mind

Popping profusely   small shoots of glimmering
   interest

              can you feel   the inner nudge?
   Something wants to grow
 needs sun   pressing up between blades of grass

        you thought
          were your real thoughts

Cross the Sea

A girl in Gaza
  speaks into a table microphone:
Do you believe in infinity?
  If so, what does it look like to you?

Not like a wall
  Not like a soldier with a gun
Not like a ruined house
    bombed out of being
Not like concrete wreckage
    of a school's good hope
        a clinic's best dream
In fact not like anything
  imposed upon you and your family
        thus far
    in your precious thirteen years.

My infinity would be
  the never-ending light
you deserve
  every road opening up in front of you.

Soberly she nods her head.

In our time   voices cross the sea
               easily
but sense is still difficult to come by.

Next girl's question:
    Were you ever shy?

To Babies

May polar bears welcome you
to northern Manitoba, their lumbering grace
marking the ice. May there still be ice.
May giant trees lean over your path
in warm places, brush your brow.
So many details now disappeared . . .
tiny toads in deserts, fireflies.
Where are the open window screens,
whispers of breeze against a sleeping cheek?
If we stop poking holes in soil,
    watching onions grow,
what will we know? If we no longer learn cursive,
will our hand muscles disintegrate?
You blink, beginning to focus.
Where will the lost loops of handwritten "*g*'s"
    and "*y*'s" go?
We dream you will have so much to admire.

Songbook

Tiny keyboard bearing the reverie of the past—
press one button, we're carried away

on a country road,

marching with saints,

leaving the Red River Valley—
here is every holiday you hated, every hard time,
every steamy summer wish. You closed your eyes,
leaned your head against a wall,

knowing a bigger world
loomed. It's still out there, and it's tucked
in this keyboard too.
Now we are an organ, now an oboe,
now we are young or ancient,
smelling the haunted wallpaper in the house
our grandfather sold with every cabinet,

table and doily included,
but we are still adrift, floating,
thrum-full of longing layers of sound.

Unsung—on Finding

From where this box of pink & purple yarns?
 Skeins not even tangled
  Recipes for baby jackets   booties
Saluting your good intentions   oh someone
   honoring your high hopes
   neatly packed in a box
     future promise   on a shelf   in our shed
     (How did this get into our shed?)
But give it away   because we know we will never
          on any day   of any future year
                    do this

Bundle

Why didn't you take a photograph
out the window of every place you ever stayed?
Clotheslines, balconies, food vendors,
could have focused on any one thing.
But I was lingering at the dock fascinated
by a seagull with a hopping gait.
Catching the breeze.
Scrap of pink ribbon,
yellow shovel half-buried in sand—

Or a picture of every classroom you inhabited,
even for an hour, the boy who said,
"I'm afraid I'm in love with the word *lyrical*,"
on a hundred-degree day,
pencil swooping across page.
He looked like the toughest customer in town
till he said that.

To wake with a word   *Bundle*
tucked between lips, and wonder all day
what it means . . . bundle of joys, troubles . . .

each day the single mystery-word could change.
Veil. Forget. Abandon.

And consider the people at any crossing walk,
   how you will never cross with them again,
isn't that enough to make a charm?

Or the careful ways we arrange a desk
   wherever we stay,
temporary landscape—pencils, sharpener,
drifting moon of a cup over everything, silent and
humble, bearing its own hope.

Little Lady, Little Nugget Brooms

Hey Baltimore, I'll take one—
do they exist anywhere
but on this fading wall?

Not all we love is gone, oh
Hunter & Elsie's Café!
Find a ghost sign
for proof. Every disappeared menu
seeding your bones. Karam's Mexican
Restaurant, more like an oasis it was,
west side San Antonio,
giant palms in back garden,
massive Aztec heads,
Ralph Karam's cozy dream
wrecked for a Walgreen's,
but can you still taste
the crackly corn chalupa
distinctiveness? Did not taste
like anywhere else.

Kalamazoo,

     meandering around in you

at dawn, on a street

with real buildings older than

  my grandpa,

  were he still alive,

the Michigan Newsstand was well-lit

  and ready to serve,

thousands of pages of new reading matter,

books, magazines,

   step right up, believe in me,

and the whispery sign on the side of a building

    Rooms for Rent 1 dollar hot supper

put my modern flying heart back in my body.

Welcome What Comes

1

Bearing secrets
underlying meanings
parallel possibility
hint of distance
company for the journey
doorstep treasure
gift wrapped loosely in bandanna
trail of ribbons
no address attached
traveling a long time over rocky terrain
trusting you were waiting

2

Some people grew up receiving no messages at all
    but from people right in front of them.
Clean your room   Wash your hands
        Homework!

Black phone in hallway nook rang so rarely,
    it shocked us when it sang—
Grandma on birthdays, lonely insurance salesman.

No disembodied messages chirping up continuously

    see this, read that, don't miss . . . how did we

        live?

We knew what was going on.

         Always felt connected.

Tonight I wanted to return

    to the days of someone telling me what to do.

At least then I thought I knew.

3

My old friend writes a real letter in the mail

    I have not yet learned how to live, have you?

  Wind still whips around our chimneys

      Sunrises feel more precious

  A blind dog wanders all night through fields

    returning home next morning wet and

exhausted

    to wrap his paws around his person's neck

What Happens Next

Ferguson, no one ever heard of you.

Unless they lived in Florissant, or Cool Valley,

we said "St. Louis" when we went away because

you were obscure, tucked in leafy green,

lost to humidity.

Sure, we could count on things—

farmer Al in baggy overalls, boxing tomatoes,

patient books lined at the library,

Hermit Lady sunken into tilting house.

Catholic pal said I could not step into his church

to see the painted statues, God would not approve,

I was not baptized, a drifter among

Ferguson's ditches and trees.

We might have guessed your coming troubles,

white teacher reading Langston with a

throaty catch in her voice. The invisible line,

Kinloch on the other side. See that word? *Kin* in it.

Made no sense to kids. Only grown-ups saw the line.

We loved your fragrances and musky soil—

everyone so poor a dime or quarter could change a day,

but filled with longing—how to spend our bounty?

My Arab daddy always wanted to know more.
Evenings we watered the grass, the trees.
Driving slowly around "the other side,"
he waved at everyone, people called him reckless,
only Arab in town got away with curiosity.
Something had to be better than
the separations humans make—
at four, I am climbing steep stairs
of the house next door.
If I sit quietly, the teenager who lives inside
will emerge and brush my hair.
She presses hard, down to the scalp.
I belong to her too.

Everything Changes the World

Boys kicking a ball on a beach,
women with cook pots,
men bombing tender patches of mint.

There is no righteous position.
Only places where brown feet
touch the earth.

Maybe you call it yours.
Maybe someone else runs it.
What do you prefer?

We who are far
stagger under the mind blade.
Every crushed home,
every story worth telling.
Think how much you'd need to say
if that were your friend.

If one of your people
equals hundreds of ours,
what does that say about people?

Standing Back

If this is the best you can do, citizens of the world,
I resolve to become summer shadow,
turtle adrift in a pool.
Today a frog waited in a patch of jasmine
for drizzles of wet before dawn.
The proud way he rose when water
touched his skin—
his simple joy at another morning—
compare this to bombing,
shooting, wrecking,
in more countries than we can count
and ask yourself—human or frog?

Three Hundred Goats

In icy fields.
Is water flowing in the tank?
(Is it the year of the sheep or the goat?
    Chinese zodiac inconclusive . . .)
Will they huddle together, warm bodies pressing?
O lead them to a secluded corner,
little ones toward bulkier mothers.
Lead them to the brush, which cuts the wind.
Another frigid night swooping down—
Aren't you worried about them, I ask my friend,
who lives by herself on the ranch of goats,
far from here near the town of Ozona.
She shrugs, "Not really,
they know what to do. They're goats."

Lost People

"The blue bird carries the sky on his back."
—Henry David Thoreau, unpublished works

For years I looked for my lost friend. We did so
much mischief together,
     made our own tiny language, wore overalls,
walked twenty miles—

when someone else's mother said we would
"get over" Henry David Thoreau,
          we knew it was not true.

               Finally—"Your previous letter
arrived,
          but I kept it many months without answering
   so it seemed to get longer. Sorry—it grew too long
to answer
so I never . . . did."

Once we were dandelion fluff
     raggedy blue jeans
   quoting Henry under yellow bell esperanza trees.

Everything already happening
rush   sizzle   miracle of becoming on
earth & we would not miss one note.
Steeped in quietude   buzzing joy
that could never fall onto a
to-do list
dish soap   paper clips

Write her a short note now—
only sky   between the words

Broken

What was precious—flexing.
Fingers wrapping bottle, jar,
fluent weave of tendon, bone, and nerve.
To grip a handle, lift a bag of books,
button simply, fold a card—
I did not feel magnificent.

Unthinking movement, come again.
These days of slow reknitting,
stoked with pain . . .
"Revise the scene of injury in your mind,"
suggested Kathleen, so then I did not
snap against the root, but just became it.
Thank your ankles, thank your wrists.
How many gifts have we not named?

Twilight

Victor the taxi driver says
I love this time of day
This is when I say
Never want to die
want to be here forever
Oh maybe it will be possible,
in the shaggy heads of trees
that barely felt us
walking beneath them
The corners we turned so often
broken pavements
cracks & signatures
Daniel Lozano 1962
All the days we entered thoughtlessly
forgetting to turn our heads or bow
to the vine finally making it over the fence

dangling blossom
orange cup of joy
ephemeral as we were
here
imagining our deep roots

VOICES IN THE AIR

People do not pass away.

They die

and then they stay.

For Aziz

I had not noticed
the delicate yellow flower
strikingly thin petals
like a man with many hopes
or a woman with many dreams
the center almost a tiny hive
ants could crawl in and out of
if they wished

Had not noticed the profusion
of flowers on the path
Had not stooped
to absorb the silent glory
of many-petaled yellow
or remembered the freshness
of my father's collar
for some years now
the rush of anticipation
circling his morning self
despite so much hard history
and searing news

Who can help us?
Yellow beam
spiral sunshine
legacy

Sheep by the Sea
a painting by Rosa Bonheur (1865)

The calm of your wool, rounded resting postures,
    hooves tucked under.
Behind you, roiling waves pound, whitecaps against
    stones.
Your eyes have been closed for a hundred and
    forty-eight years.
But you seem not to fear what is coming. You curl in
    repose,
Pink velvet of your ears echoing the pink tips of the
    grasses.
People have always been shepherds for sheep,
    but I'd like
to let you lead. Quiet depth, a measured gentleness.
Here in a museum in Washington, D. C.

Emily

What would you do if you knew
that even during wartime
scholars in Baghdad
were translating your poems
into Arabic
still believing
in the thing with feathers?

You wouldn't feel lonely
That's for sure.

Words finding friends
even if written on envelope flaps
or left in a drawer.

Warbler Woods

For Peter Matthiessen

Never too proud to tip his head back.
To gaze, look beyond.
Something nesting in leaves, unseen,
presence on a boulder beside water,
single strong leg.
Fine if it took a long time to walk there.
Better if it took time . . .

He knew the names of every warbler,
stitched inside his skin,
the seven eagles, graceful cranes, he followed them
to tucked-away forests and creeks, could see
a slightest flicker of movement,
a nesting memory, how the world was once,
would never be again.
He could stand under skies for hours,
never weary of their habits, never tire.

When did humans equal this glory?
Glory of feather and snippet.

Glory of the rangeless distances—
abundant glide.
When did humans soar so high?

Gratitude Pillow

"Let gratitude be the pillow upon which you kneel . . ."
            —Maya Angelou

Maya loved the jingle of the massive key ring
carried by cable car conductors. First woman
in the San Francisco trolley uniform,
she liked the shiny buttons on the jacket,
appreciated the swoops and dips of the routes,
sharp curves, corners, bustling avenues.
Clinking coin dispenser latched to her belt,
she'd be a conductor all her life. Write, and talk,
take people everywhere, out of their tight little
    rooms.
And if anyone told her they were going
to Gloomy Street,
she'd say, What? Lift those eyes. Take a look at the
sea to your right, buildings full of mysteries, schools
crackling with joy, open porches,
watch the world whirl by,

all we are given without having to own, and shake

that gloom right out of your system!

Hope is the only drink you need

to be drinking—jingle, jingle, step right up.

Life Loves

to change, wrote poet John Masefield,
in the cobbled town of Ledbury, Herefordshire,
Elizabeth Barrett Browning's town too.
  Precise crosswalks, Saturday cheese markets,
hourly church bells bonging with conviction.
A man called Ledbury one of the few "real towns"
left in England, meaning—sad to say—they don't
have many immigrants. (Took me a week to figure
    this out.)
      Too bad, for it was easy to imagine
              hiding out down Cottage Lane behind
          massive white roses for years,
paper-wrapped hunk of greasy fish and chips
    on the iron garden table. Who knows how many
lives long for any one of us? Who else we might be?
  We're thirsty for a cider shop's thirty faucets,
no idea which is best. Whatever you say! We're not
headed to Hope's End, where Elizabeth lived, we're
awash in Hope's Beginnings.
Haunting the old-fashioned print shop, plucking
sheaves of discarded margins from rubbish bin—

long thin creamy strips—
basking in disgusted teen chatter
on the green by the graveyard,
    holding the air. It became my air too quickly.
I felt drunk on general coziness . . .
    thinking of Elizabeth,
whose "father never spoke to her again," once she
had a child (what was his problem?),
and Masefield, who suffered intense seasickness
    yet wrote about going down to the sea
      as if it were his favorite act.

Walking everywhere, pausing for slow crossing lights,
    nodding conspiratorially to ladies with canes
hiking hill path at dawn . . .
    Life loves to change—but some of us want to
stay.

〜〜

Getting Over It

Years ago, the writer and translator Coleman Barks
& I met up in Rome, Georgia, a town that had once
been the home of his grandmother, to eat Chinese
food with friends. He drove us to the restaurant. I
was on a nine-day poetry tour of Georgia, filling in
for someone who had cancelled at the last moment.
The sheriff of Macon had attended my reading & told
me his real dream was to be a writer. The Branch
Davidians in Waco had just burned up. I was lugging
my canvas poetry bag stuffed with books & papers
into the restaurant.

Coleman said, Why drag that? Leave it in the car! It
will be safe!

No, I said. Everything I need is in this bag. I keep it
right next to me.

That is ridiculous, he said. No one will take a bag of
books.

We ate a delicious dinner & upon returning to the car, discovered it had been broken into & Coleman's own bag taken—which contained his books, personal journal, plane ticket to Turkey for the next week, passport, drawings by his granddaughter—many treasures.

He was shocked. He said something about my worry having attracted negative attention to the vehicle. He wasn't blaming, just musing. I said I wasn't worried, really—I always lugged my bag.

Coleman called the police. They looked around vaguely & loaned us a giant flashlight, saying we could return it to the police station the next day.

A whirl of awkward searching through weedy ditches & smelly Dumpsters turned up nothing. We kept looking & hoping, in case the thieves had ransacked Coleman's bag for money, then thrown the rest of it away.

We searched into the night.

I got angrier on Coleman's behalf as the search went on, but he grew calmer. How can people take what isn't theirs? I thought about refugees, my father, women who are attacked unexpectedly, then have to accommodate that brutal shock into the future, too many things. Coleman apparently kept his mind on the bag.

Around midnight, he said, "How long does one stay robbed, after being robbed? I think I'm over it."

He drove me back to the house where I was spending the night. My friendly host, artist and writer Susan Gilbert Harvey, was still awake. She thought we might have been abducted. I told her what had happened & what Coleman said, which caused us to suspend our search. Susan burst into tears.

She said, "That's it. That's it exactly. That's what I've been needing to hear. Such a gift!"

Conversation with Grace Paley, Flight of the Mind Writing Workshop, Oregon

It's been a spectacular day, Grace!

We gushed

And she cleared her throat.

Not that great, she said—

But pretty good.

Didn't you like our long drive into the woods

      to see trees with rounded buttocks?

They were okay.

Our splendid dinner?

Tasty.

Grace, guide us! What is politics to you?

You are such a brave activist!

How do we live, what do we do?

Politics is simply the way human beings treat

one another on the earth.

Showing Up
For Lucille Clifton

Where else would I be? said Lucille, after surgeries
and months of pain, where else? She swooped back
into action, visiting with students, attending readings,
sending out her beams. Some people are born
    to be present, hold the note.
Shape a mouth around words, air them fully,
      convince others they could do this too.

    We're such skinny souls sometimes,
brimming with excuses for inaction,
     passing the blame.
           Lucille's own daddy had said,
"All good-byes ain't gone"—and she carried that
truth—

    Hello again!—even when she'd been laid up in
hospital for a while. Never mind!
     Picture the whirl of energy
           beneath each human move—
    circulating, rising with every
step. Lucille stayed late, singing the song of
      carrying on, admitting the truth . . .

"Things don't fall apart. Things hold. Lines connect in thin ways that last and last . . ."

Lucille gave everything she had.

For Caroline M.

What does it mean when, across fifty years and a

thousand miles, a voice literally reaches out of the sky,

Naomi! I did it! Good-bye!

and you dial rapidly, last number you had for her,

to find the nurses scrambling, since they haven't

    even reached her brother yet,

and you say, *Now! Now! Let me speak to her!*

and they say, *You can't!*

so you know she just wanted to alert you,

have you as witness she finally broke free,

same way she used to announce

she was driving into town

in the rattled truck with the crushed bumper—

Good-bye! Try to finish up those rows before you leave,

okay?

so you'd know she still had her eye on you

always watching even when she wasn't present—

you were the only girl at the farm, except for her.

Caroline and her husband, whom you worked for at
    twelve,
attempting to impress them with your berry-picking
    skills,
tin can looped around your neck. She wasn't sure you
could stand it, spoken day one, but grew impressed
by your love for heat, your trance-like gathering.

Years later, whenever you returned to town,
you always stopped to hike up the dirt drive
into sweet-soil-smelling paradise,
flag of honest organic farming
growing more precious in the world.
Caroline, I still love your tomatoes, don't you?

I hate tomatoes, they smell like work.

Also, I never liked farming, you know, I only loved him.
What?
I was a city girl. Or wanted to be.
Seriously?
More layers than anyone can see,

roots threading into soil, tightening the grip,
leaving you standing on the land years after she
called you without a phone, whispering,
Blackberries, tomatoes.
Thank you.
I'm home.

Tomorrow

For José Emilio Pacheco who said, "I like poetry to be the interior voice, the voice no one hears, the voice of the person reading it."

1

What animal is waiting to hear what we have to say?
Not one. Not the red-winged blackbird,
the speckled trout

or the French Chartreux. Beg an iguana
for editorial advice.
Whatever we do, slim drift on the wind.

We could talk forever, never equaling the dawn song
of the thrush.
Pacheco said, "Fish don't torture. Their banks don't
ever charge interest."

We open our mouths.
We find and hide the words.

2

My friend who knew him says, "I thought of him
as a businessman only. A lawyer? Had no idea he
wrote poems."
She found him dignified, stately, quiet.
Papers, envelopes, nice neckties, polished desk.

José Emilio, your "certain silences"
were invisible girders.
They held everything up. Childhood stories,
first moments, ". . . we go never to come back."
No wonder you translated Beckett, Yevtushenko . . .
belonging to other worlds deepened our own.
You wanted to ask your old teachers if the Future—
"Tomorrow"—
lived up to their dreams. Everyone's hard work,
supposed to count for everything, right?
Who predicted torture, murder, people
disappeared?

Didn't those people work hard too?
Which animals live like this?
Could metaphor soothe or save?
There are nine moths to every one butterfly.

Your poems at first surrealistic, then closer to home.
Fancy awards, dramatic titles, did not intrigue.
Your pants fell down when meeting a king, but you
hiked them up, calling it a cure for vanity.
We love you forever for moments like this.
Leaning into your pages all those years—
working and working. "All that is truly ours now
is the day that is beginning." Once we gleaned what
went on in high places—
our job to build something better.

After Listening to Paul Durcan, Ireland

"Should there be anyone who has not got mixed feelings?
Could there be anyone who has not got mixed feelings?"

Poured full of ripe language
but no mixed feelings about
how much we adore him
we lift into night
buttery streetlamp glow
gray sweaters and topcoats
unbuttoned at the throat
pearls and nubby mufflers
tonight the cream of understanding
elevated elegance of sound
funny quirky joy
two neighbors who never met before
meet in a doctor's office and end up befriending
each other same way you could hear poems
and feel restored to clear notes
so when we step into the street
taxis bunching and idling

bowed heads

silent grins

we have those notes to go by

deeper current

streaming into the fluent dark

We Will Get Lost in You

"You forget everything when you play—that's why you do it, actually."

        —Leo Kottke, guitarist

Joni Mitchell said in an interview, Everything I am,
I'm not.
Bigger. Smaller. Entirely invisible. A painter, not a
musician.
Secrets you never dreamed. Somewhere else.
Tish jumped over a fence. Tish narrated a story—
where people went when they disappeared, inside
your own skin.
Lay your burden down—no, dissolve your burden!
Not your burden! Bruce kept singing from
an engine deep inside.
We could walk the halls where Robert Johnson walked.
Patty Griffin, *The further I go*,
more letters from home never arrive. Not to be lost.
Amidst millions of people, calm sanctuaries of sound
in Tokyo, beyond the Sad Café,
Joanna Newsom's high notes

weaving harp trills, lifting a crowd to the ceiling.

Or Minnesota when winter was nearly over,

Sara Thomsen stomping, Too many roosters

in the White House! Yep. Spirits in time of disaster.

You! Can do it when you open your mouth, right?

There Will Be a Light, when politicians lie,
    people insult,

when you didn't want to read the comments on a
    story but did,

and can't stop wondering why people take time to be
    cruel,

when they could be all those other things,

baby beating drum on a box, train clatter braking
    into station,

pluck the string of the day and go away.

James Tate in Jerusalem

A writer whose lines could "ambush with wonder
    and wit"
saved me once. In the rugged hills outside Jerusalem,
I was reeling with sadness, as usual, my people
    pressed like cattle
by sharp butts of Israeli guns, herded through
battered lines, endlessly insulted,
(I wanted to fix it, always a problem, or translate us
all into a better world),
when a guide climbed on our bus wearing
a FREE TIBET T-shirt.
Jim just looked at me. He saw it too.
"That's thoughtful."
Something cracked.
Sanity ambushed day after day. His kindness
made a calm place in my fury.
He drank a Pepsi. I seethed.
His words cool and angled, pieced together like
triangles in a quilt stitched by the calm Amish.
Blue and green don't fight.

Trust me. We have sunk so low in this valley of repetition we forgot how to sew a seam.

Train Across Texas
For Langston Hughes

Langston, what did Texas look like back then,
    where were you going?
From your seat on the train, the small table,
you encouraged your pen pals,
timid Baltimore sisters,
who had shared their writing with you,
and no one else.
           Sure you can do it. You are doing it!
    Sent them gloriously handwritten
black-inked letters . . .
sentences trailing across pages on neat tracks—
     drew pictures in margins—hills outside the
window,
a dining car waiter with a white towel folded over his
   arm.
You had time on your beautiful ride, so much space
to stare into, horizons of thinking.
    I believe in you. Don't let anyone tell you
                   otherwise.
You knew what it was to be a busboy, wipe tables,

contemplate crusts, dregs of tea in a cup.
Urging your pen pals to remember their dreams
whatever shape they might be.
You were ready for the next installment . . . there
were ways to get anywhere you wanted to go,
if you really want to go.

And the land opened up in front of you.
              The long land.
And the years in which you would be writing to
every one of us
every day.

Longfellow's Bed
For Henry Wadsworth Longfellow

seems too short for a man, especially one with
such a name, but they say it stretches six feet.
Dark wooden sleigh with coverlets,
bed to dive into, in another century,
to hide in, beyond flame and sorrow,
bed with large pillows to comfort
an aching trove of rhythms and syllables,
down by the Charles River we will go
when daylight shines. I wish I had known you,
Longfellow, but truly I did, as a small reader
with a book cracked wide, speaking aloud
on the old wooden stairs of my grandparents' home,
saying your words, *between the daylight*
and the dark, swinging them like small lanterns
which have brought me to this place
by your bed on a late day in June,
in your yellow house by the giant linden tree,
still wondering at words and the length of a mattress.

Walt Whitman's Revisions

"Transcendent! New! An American bard at last!"
(written about himself and his major life work, *Leaves of Grass*)

Trim the grass

Feed the grass

Water the grass

Direct the grass

This parched lawn　　　needs attention

What started as skinny chapbook

of twelve poems

grew into four hundred

in forty years

Who has such fortitude?

Walt was always working on the same book

First edition did not

have his name on cover

He reviewed himself in newspapers anonymously

quoted Ralph Waldo Emerson

without permission

on the spine

Emerson was not thrilled

Take a breath

Full breath

That's what I call a poet

"Rest and Be Kind,
You Don't Have to Prove Anything"

For Jack Kerouac, who said this was his best advice for writers

In 1972 I sat with Stella Kerouac in her St.
Petersburg, Florida, home thinking, "I can't believe
I'm really here, sitting in Jack's lounger, Jack's cat
nuzzling my foot, I can't believe she let me in, I can't
believe she's putting these papers in my hands."

Stella, who met Jack as a child. He was her
younger brother's friend. She said it felt like only
moments since Jack had died, though already it
had been a few years. She wanted me to read some
unpublished pieces of Jack's fluent prose into a tape
recorder. She was making an oral archive and thought
her own voice, after years of smoking, too coarse
for posterity. My hands trembled as I recorded his
words, thinking, "This is a page he really touched."
She thought papers might disappear, but cassette tapes
were going to last forever.

Some sweet, quick link had been established
between Stella and me weeks earlier, when I
telephoned her from Texas on my forlorn twentieth

birthday (also Jack's birthday), let the phone ring at least twenty times, and finally heard her tearful "Hello?" I babbled into the phone, tentatively at first, since I'd heard she was reclusive. I expected her to hang up at any moment. She didn't hang up. She said she'd been kneeling by Jack's bed missing him on his birthday, wondering if anyone anywhere might be thinking about him right then. Perfect timing. I couldn't stop thinking about him. She invited me to come visit her.

My parents drove me down. I was going to take the bus, but they were always so good about driving me. The library? Violin lessons? Jack Kerouac's house in Florida? Sure, let's drive.

They dropped me off and went away to the beach. For a few days Stella and I talked, ate tuna fish, pawed through closets, and didn't answer the phone. The phone rang frequently, but she wouldn't touch it. "It's his phone, not mine," she said. Indeed, the phone was still listed under Jack Kerouac in the directory, which was how I had found her. We used to call Information. There was no answering machine.

Jack's mother, Gabrielle, still living in a back bedroom, shook a tinny bell for attention. Stella rushed off to see what she needed. Trays of food and lemonade traveled to the bedroom and returned empty. I wanted to meet Gabrielle very much, but Stella said she was "beyond meeting people." Gabrielle sent her greetings to me out in the front room, signed a little navy blue Christmas chapbook by Jack for me, and said to take it easy.

Stella fed their cats at the kitchen table as if they were people. She set places for them. They sat on high stools, putting their mouths up to their plates. We sat at either end of the table. It seemed natural while we were doing it.

Later she would try to give me the gray kitten of one of Jack's cats. I loved this idea. We had many phone conversations about how the cat might be sent from Florida to Texas—I recall discussing a bus trip, but the cat could not travel by itself. A plane was expensive. The whole operation seemed too stressful a prospect for the kitten, however we imagined it, and was never accomplished.

Then the phone in their kitchen rang again. This

time, Stella told me to answer it. I fumbled the receiver. "Hello?"

"Who's this?" said a faraway voice.

"I'm visiting Stella," I stuttered.

"Well, put her on, would you? This is Allen Ginsberg."

When I said, "Allen Ginsberg," Stella put her hand out. She talked to him. She was friendly. I thought about the reading he'd given at our college in Texas that year, incense adrift on the air, his harmonium humming. We'd all gone into a sandalwood poetry trance, sitting with legs crossed, smiling back at him. Never had I imagined I'd be sitting in Kerouac's house when I heard his voice again.

As Stella handed the receiver back to me to hang it up, she sighed and said, "That Allen . . . I can always tell when it's Allen. It has a different ring."

Peace Pilgrim's Pocket

How old are you, Peace?
    I am *ageless*!

Only three things in her pocket
comb   toothbrush   postage stamps
With those three possessions she lived
    so many (secret number) years
making millions of friends
    hiking byways and back roads
  crossing the nation again and again
town to town thousands of miles
    unafraid
Life is a mirror!
Smile at it, it smiles back!
  woman with a white bun
    striding by herself in a navy blue tunic
  white tennis shoes
    no money no credit cards no tickets
opening her mouth wherever people would listen
    Never stop your efforts for peace!
walking till someone offered a bed

fasting till they offered food
Personal peace necessary before world peace!
Every good thing you say . . . vibrates on and on
                    and never ceases!
I am standing outside under ageless pecan trees
        listening to the voice I first heard in my
parents' living room
                as a girl of three
        Would you kill a cow?
            The three-year-old said, Never!
Then how can you eat meat?
Why let someone else do your dirty work for you?
She was thrilled to turn kids into vegetarians
I'm only a little person but
        there are lots of little things to be done!

C. D. Stepped Out

"I believe words are golden as goodness is golden. Even the
humble word *brush* gives off a scratch of light."
　　　　—C. D. Wright

C. D. stepped out into the dark.
Didn't tell anyone she was going—
she just left.
Some of us thought she was inside
in the bathroom on the second floor,
so we waited for her.
Some of us thought she was in the backyard
on a metal chair, listening.
Dark Street, MacDougal at Houston—
old furniture piled on sidewalks—
rooms of light in ancient brick buildings—
somehow she had inhabited every one
of those rooms one time or another.
She heard the twining chorus of accents,
carried them with her, rolling in her cells,
heard the roll and clash of citizens,
layerings of rooms draped with old India print,
Japanese kimono cloth, some rustic basket weave of

putty grays.

It was time, enough of this talk,

I heard you all, heard you better

than you heard me maybe, never mind, we'll catch

up later,

I just had to go.

True Success

"To travel hopefully is a better thing than to arrive . . . "
—Robert Louis Stevenson

The *hau* tree under which you wrote holds fast
      at Sans Souci Beach.
Memory curled in sap and cells—people now sit
in your favorite shade, near Waikiki,
drinking pinkish cocktails,
eating elegantly designed plates of rice and fish . . .
but the presence of one tall thin Scottish man
    with a debonair mustache,
      who leaned over his page, right here,
        . . . feels more real.

Once you were packing your leather valise in old
    gray Edinburgh—
      farewell to the fireplace, the daily chill rain, the
          cough.
You dreamed of ships, currents, a warm pause with a
horizon on it—
      already you'd written Jekyll and Hyde in a week,
        and the poem about lying abed on pillows,

creating a country of toys in the sheets,

    that would comfort sick children for decades.

When you, Robert (your wife called you "Louis"),

    arrived for a time on O'ahu—ink pen and hat—

you quickly made a new life in a gangly bungalow

      on Queen Emma Street,

        preferring soft rain against misty green

mountains,

clean bright air, sailboats—to the colder worlds you

    had known.

Writing outside in sun under a twisty tree became

    your refuge.

      "True success is to labor," you said.

        Though you died at forty-four,

    who does more than what you did?

    Making pages that would live so long . . . islands

as treasures . . .

      human lives as treasures . . .

you took a deep breath,

    opened your packet of cheese and fruit, curled into

    the words.

        These branches still rustle.

Woven by Air, Texture of Air

"Your job is to find out what the world is trying to be."
—William Stafford

Some birds hide in leaves so effectively
you don't see they're all around you.
Brown tilted heads, observing human maneuvers
on a sidewalk. Was that a crumb someone threw?
Picking and poking, no fanfare for company,
gray huddle on a branch, blending in.
Attention deeper than a whole day.
Who says, I'll be a thoughtful bird when I grow up?
Stay humble, blend, belong to all directions.
Fly low, love a shadow. And sing, sing freely,
never let anything get in the way of your singing,
not darkness, not winter,
not the cries of flashier birds, not the silence
that finds you steadfast
pen ready, at the edge of four a.m.
Your day is so wide it will outlive everyone.
It has no roof, no sides.

Tell Us All the Gossip You Know

(How I was introduced at a writer's club in small-town USA)

Gulp.
I'm a reader not a gossiper.
But we know you know some. So tell it.
Gulp.

⌒

Robert Bly said writing a bad poem before breakfast
every day is a good habit.
He did it in honor of his old friend Bill Stafford
(who also did it) after Bill died.
The poems were never bad, by the way.
They were great.
There were a lot of them.
You could work on them later, after you ate.

⌒

Leonard Nathan, chairman of the Department of
    Rhetoric

at UC Berkeley, worried computers might diminish one's investment in a line. If you could just erase the line instantly, and insert a new one—
well, it might be too easy.

~

Mary Oliver wanted to smell flowering pink bushes and blossoming trees in Texas.
Pull over, she said, at more than one corner. She needed to absorb the scents.
A city wasn't just a name.
In her presence, babies might sing for the first time. She is like that.

~

Ernest Hemingway ate an apple before writing.
This might or might not have explained his crisp, short sentences.
In the house where he died in Idaho, his shaving cream still sits inside the medicine cabinet.

~

Ruth Stone wore a pale shimmering prom dress
from—1930?—1940?—
to her poetry reading in Texas in the 1990s.
She said the dress was lonely hanging in her closet
and wanted to be used.

∼

Josephine Miles, who traveled with her wheelchair
around the country to read poems,
said, Don't make your poem a neat package with a
bow tied at the end. She also said,
It's hard to help.

∼

Anyone can visit Walt Whitman's birthing corner on
Long Island.
The guide points and says, There, right there, he was
born.
Some visitors can't move on quickly
to the next room.
They are hypnotized.
What if Walt had never left this corner or stepped out

into the streets
    to do and say all he did?
Then who would we be?

~

Genine Lentine said she'd like to ban the word
"flow"—I don't understand this
but respect her, so think about it. What's wrong with
"flow"? Are your thoughts
flowing? Your words flowing? What's up with this,
Genine?
She does not care
for haiku.

~

William Burroughs also believed in taking Vitamin
C.

~

Ken Kesey wore a Mexican serape and said Jack
Kerouac got trapped in his "own little

box"—that was his downfall. Can we really say
anyone who changed so many lives
had a downfall?
He just drank too much alcohol and had a shorter life
than he might have had.
Jack's box was pretty vast.

2

William Goyen said writing started with trouble—
what you never worked out yet—just start there.
That thing in the street when you were seventeen?
Make it a story.

2

There is only one known video of Mark Twain,
wearing a white linen suit in 1909,
walking outside a house in Connecticut,
talking with Thomas Edison.

2

Daria Donnelly's last essay was about "literature of
empathy." Why we need it in our crazy world.
Don't put any Americans in your story for American
kids, maybe.
Don't make them heroes or villains, if you do.
On her tombstone she wanted
NEVER TASTED COCA-COLA.

∼

Garth Williams got a letter from his close friend
Margaret Wise Brown after she died.
It traveled from Europe so it took a while.

∼

When I visited Emily Dickinson's house in Amherst,
a lively plump robin was sitting on her step,
right under the second-story window she would have
stared out of.

∼

John Steinbeck
would sharpen
twenty-four pencils every day
and write
till they were
dull.

Every Day

For Aziz, and Palestine

He loved the world and what might happen in it.
Some people labor to get up but
he was so ready to rise.
Refreshed and still alive
after the dark hours,
glistening with hope and cologne.
Must we love the world doubly much now
in his absence?

He is not absent.
Still living in the fig tree,
the carefully placed stone,
the draping mimosa.
In his empty notebooks, the lonely wooden chair.
We will keep it pulled up to the desk, just in case.
Just in case Justice suddenly walks into the room and
says, Yes, I'm finally here, sorry for the delay.
Tell me where to sign.
He tried to think the best of people.
His drawer was not stacked with disappointments.

Only folded white handkerchiefs still waiting.
After the storm, frogs and toads chorus along the pavement,
We believed! We believed!

One State

"I see no other way than to begin now to speak about sharing the land that has thrust us together and sharing it in a truly democratic way, with equal rights for each citizen."
—Dr. Edward Said

Hiding place inside the early hour—

You're there.

Fold in the sky's softest cloth—

what rises as we sleep,

the dark and ripe and narrow wedge.

You dropped every list of activities.

You're off the hook.

And who are we?

Slice of the deep, hanging on hard.

Trying to do honor.

Situations getting worse.

Bumbling pie.

Hello, good morning, guess what,

you didn't die.

My Name Is . . .

Their silence
is bigger
than our silence.
Chief Joseph
did not wish to go to Kansas.
He said, I think very little of this country.
It is like a poor man. It amounts to nothing.
Of course we realize a poor man can amount
to anything, Jesus was a poor man,
Gandhi, but Chief Joseph
had been kicked out of his valley, away from his
gleaming Wallowa Lake, and he was burned.
To this day you cannot walk there without aching.

Look at this earth.
How many adrift.
A man-in-exile read words and phrases
copied by a Syrian refugee boy
into a notebook dredged sopping from the
Mediterranean, dried on the shore. The boy was
learning more words every day

before he went down, improving

his vocabulary, coming to a new world,

for safety and rescue. Please Madame, my name is

Abdul,

this is my family, my brother, my sister, I am happy

to know you.

Invitation to the NSA

Feel free to scrutinize my messages. Welcome. Have
fun fanning through my private thoughts on drones,
the Israeli Army chopping down olive trees, endless
wars in Iraq and Afghanistan, horrific from the get-
go, and we told you so, but no one listened because
there was a lot of money and oomph in it, so feel free
to listen now. Bombs have no mothers. That is an
insult to mothers. See what I think about Bashar
al-Assad vs. the children of Syria, pass it on, please,
or weapons in general, the George W. Bush library in
Dallas which I refused to drive my mother past. I like
the sense of you looking over our shoulders, lifting
up the skirts of our pages, peering under my fury
at how you forget Palestine again and again, forget
the humble people there, never calling them the
victimized innocents as you call others. You forget
your promises, forget religion, *Thou Shalt Not Kill,*
and yet you kill, in so many ways, so what do we
care? You might as well see what we say.

Double Peace

For Yehuda Amichai

"If I try to be like him, who will be like me?"—Yiddish proverb

Not for him and his people alone
  but for all who loved that rocky land
Everybody everybody sing it!
No chosen and unchosen but everybody chosen
   Sing it!
All families living under tiled rooftops
Or flat roofs with strung clotheslines
  T-shirts bedsheets flags of surrender
I show you my cloth I live the way you live
All the cousins second cousins
   extra cousins unknown cousins
No choice everyone a cousin
  peace better than hurtful moves
   better better sing it!
Not rain that fell on a few houses only
   Not sun that shone on a few favored yards
Not air in small containers only for some lungs
   Double peace multiplied
Outside inside every ancient space

every sleek new room with tall windows

Peace for sheep and goats grazing in meadows

   (They already have it)

   Peace for buckets waiting on doorsteps

Peace in brown eggs lined on counters waiting to be

                    cracked

   Peace in skillets and spatulas

We met at the corner   went to his home for

                    breakfast

He said, I would never have taken your father's

                    home!

   I could never have lived in a stolen Arab home!

   The great voice of the Jewish people said this to

my face

             our conversation

                where streets converged

Break the Worry Cocoon

"Take them, use them, I beg you to travel."
                    —Samih al-Qasim, from "Travel Tickets"

To live with what we are given—
graciously, as if our windows open wide as our
neighbors', as if there weren't insult at every turn.
How did you do that?

" . . . if social justice will be victorious in all the
world . . . I don't care who will remember me or my
poems."

You sprang from the earth same way everyone does,
from the soil of your parents, the small bed and
hopeful song.
Were pressed along through a century
that didn't honor your people,
who washed their faces anyway,
stitched the dresses, buttoned shirts.

" . . . travel tickets . . . one to peace . . .
one to the fields and the rain, and one to the

conscience of humankind . . ."
How did you survive so much hurt and remain
gracious,
finding words to mark the shapes
of grief, how did you believe,
then and forever, breaking out
of the endless worry cocoon,
something better might come your people's way?

The Tent

When did hordes of sentences start
beginning with So—
as if everything were always pending,
leaning on what came before.
What can you expect?
Loneliness everywhere, entertained or kept in
storage.
So you felt anxious to be alone.
Easier to hear, explore a city, room,
mound of hours, no one walking beside you.
Talking to self endlessly, but mostly listening.
This would not be strange.
It would be the tent you slept in.
Waking calmly inside whatever
you had to do would be freedom.
It would be your country.
The men in front of me had whole acres
in their eyes. I could feel them cross, recross each day.
Memory, stitched. History, soothed.
What we do or might prefer to do. Have done.
How we got here. Telling ourselves a story

till it's compact enough to bear.
Passing the walls, wearing the sky,
the slight bow and rising of trees.
Everything ceaselessly holding us close.
So we are accompanied.
Never cast out without a line of language
to reel us back.
That is what happened, how I got here.
So maybe. One way anyway.
A story was sewn, seed sown,
this was what patriotism meant to me—
to be at home inside my own head long enough
to accept its infinite freedom
and move forward anywhere, to mysteries coming.
Even at night in a desert, temperatures plummet,
billowing tent flaps murmur to one another.

Please Sit Down
For Vera B. Williams

Your mama will have a chair
Everyone will have a chair
There are enough chairs

In the dreams we share
desks with smooth wooden tops
Name cards in calligraphy
cubbyholes under seats
What else might people be given?

When everyone sits calmly in chairs
Numbers march across pages
Letters line up friendly-fashion

Hopefully we might like those letters enough
to shape them into stories
Where have you been before here?
Who did you see?

A woman of sturdy conviction
clear, clear focus
making history with her hands

A garden, a muffin, a world?
Greedy men say "More!" to war
Sitting together telling stories
could change that but who will take the time?
Missiles faster

All our lives to speak of simple things
turns out to be
most complicated

For the Birds

"Why not?"—Dorothy Stafford's late-life motto

Why aren't you filling your feeders these days,
my mother asks—the birds are disappointed,
they keep landing on the feeder and flying away
looking sad. And I thought about our lives,
days crammed full of doings—so many messages,
do they feed us or make us fretful?
Maybe the birds are messages
too. But saying what? We watch them landing,
ruffling succulent soft brown layered wings,
wearing snazzy yellow beaks,
and I haul out the sack of seeds.

Bowing Candles
For John O'Donohue

How lonely your house feels, like the abandoned

house of an ancient shepherd, in the far Connemara

    meadows.

Though I pictured it white, the outer walls are

    muddy brown.

We peer through windows.

    Candles on long wooden table

        bend over at their waists,

            wax softening in sun

        bowing to your absence.

Still in shock, as are we. How could your voice be so

    alive—then gone?

Nothing boxed or put away—you left unexpectedly.

        I feel shy—never having met you but

    remembering your graceful handwriting across

years of letters—

        and what did we say?

Yes of course, take it away, my poem is your poem,

    all poems belong to anyone who loves them.

        You carried light to tables—long tables

around the world like this wooden one

still waiting here—everyone remembers you—

serving light on plates with place mats.

You wrote about beauty, joy, belonging.

Quickly, someone must move into your

house.

Black Car

For Van Morrison

Everyone still resonating, sliding
saxophone, searing plume of joy that lit the hall,
coating gilt ceiling, causing us all
to rise, raise our hands.
What it is to carry a voice like that.
From side stage door to back seat of car.
Crowd still hovering cheers again,
engine zooms into night.
Thank you. Thank you. Pressing the walk button
we fly.

MORE WORLDS

"Many Indians say they live in two worlds, but
they actually have to live in more than two
worlds. If you live in one world you are pretty
much stuck in one place. Right now, I am living
in the cab-driving world, the sober world, the
Indian world, the art world. The more worlds
you live in, the better it is."

—FRANK BIG BEAR JR., ARTIST

Mountains

Jesse never felt smarter than at age six
the only first grader in a fifth-grade poetry
workshop—
when they wrote about their neighborhood
his poem by far the best in the room
and he the first volunteer to stand and read it.
The big kids clapped for him and cheered.
He remembered this at twenty-one
when we crossed paths on Commerce Street.
Hey, hey! Could I ever feel like that again?
It was my Best Day!
Now working two jobs   two kids to support
        Yes I think so
    Do you read to your kids?
    Do you have a library card?
        Do you use it?
No   No   No
Start there, Jesse! You knew the truth
when you were six   that your street was magical
and full of mountains
though it was utterly flat.

You wrote about the rooster's songs

    and the dogs' barkingful wonder.

You wrote Who do you think I am   am   am?

And knew instinctively it was more powerful to say

   "am"

three times than one—

You are still that person.

Oh, Say Can You See

I'd like to take Donald Trump to Palestine,
set him free in the streets of Ramallah or Nablus
amidst all the winners who never gave up in sixty-
nine years.
They'd like to make their country great again too,
if only their hands weren't tied by the weapons
our country donates. Let's talk about who belongs
where,
how an immigrant to Israel is treated better than
someone
who tended a tree for a hundred years. Who lies?
Let's talk about lies. Give it a shout! They built a wall
so ugly, kids must dream of flying over,
or burrowing under, and it didn't solve anything.
I'd wrap a keffiyeh around his head,
tuck some warm falafels into his pockets,
let him wander alleyways and streets,
rubble and hope mixing together,
nothing oversized, no tall towers,

just beautiful life, mint flourishing in a tin can,
schoolgirl in a fresh dress with a ruffle, mom and dad
staring from the windows—Can you see us?
Can you see any of us at all?

Anti-Inaugural

I pledge allegiance
To respect
For every one
Of you

~

Talking truth
is hard
Staying silent
should be harder

~

My voting preference?
Every person
In this city

~

Silence waits
For truth
To break it

~

You be my president,
I'll be yours

~

We have never
    paid
Enough attention
    yet

~

Some days
we are
the fallen flower

~

Abundance!
Nature doesn't shout.

Be brave
Little things
Still matter most

I Vote for You
For Connor James Nye

You smile at everyone. When lifted, toted,
you hold tightly to shoulder or sleeve.
Gazing curiously, each room, face,
Irish sheep, stuffed puppy.
Dwelling in a current of care,
you know nothing of cruelties people do
to one another.
You did not see the intricate avenues of Aleppo—
tiled ceilings, arching rooms.
The villages of Palestine
could still be neatly terraced in your brain.
When you smile, we might all be
wishing each other well.
When you startle at a loud sound,
await the power of softness
to settle you down. There is no other power
in your world.
Hunger, interest, kicking, joy—carry us there.

If your eyes fall heavily closed,

sweet rescue in the dozing.

What we might remember if we tried much harder.

In your dream no one is a refugee.

Everyone has clean sheets.

Belfast
(For Frankee & Paul)

I'm attached to everything
   things that aren't mine
places that aren't mine
     (nothing is mine)
fingers feeling for a switch in the dark
   knowing how a knob turns or sticks
after only two days
   click of the lock
    attached to swerves   surprise   new corners
riding an elevator to the seventh floor of the old
   linen mill
    meeting artists
simply by knocking on their doors
Tell again—what was all that violence for?
Old Belfast   I'm attached to your red brick
      peaks & pitches   compact neighborhoods
green slopes behind (they aren't mine)
haunting yellow cranes at the Titanic shipyard
   gray slate stones on the beach
(we could see Scotland   also not mine

but now I'm so attached to everything

     I almost doubled in size)

attached to Stranmillis Road   swans

     swifts   rivers

the glorious face of Queen's University

  we could start over

          everything over

new world   new map   new life

and the baked potato with cheese and red beans

  I kept hearing about

there is more   there is more   there is more

Summer

Up late watching TV commercials while waiting for the last quarter of the basketball finals game—it's clear what someone must think Americans want: everything to blow up. Catastrophic explosions, chaos, car chases, mobs of desperate people running from zombies, massive flying robot creatures with their weapons pointed directly at us. It is NOW SUMMER AND WE HAVE MADE THIS MOVIE FOR YOU. OPENING SOON. Even the national capitol features giant flames spilling out of its dome. These commercials will whet the appetites of fellow Americans who, only a few decades ago, were happy with lightning bugs and lemonade. What happened to us?

A Lonely Cup of Coffee

Far preferable
to a sociable cup
which tastes more
of talk
the lonely cup
redolent
rich
ripe
round
blesses
the quiet mouth

Reading Obituaries on the Day
of the Giant Moon

Is it possible to fall in love posthumously with
someone's stunningly mismatched eyebrows
and straight-on gaze?
Kazue's summary describes her as "a fiery woman
even at seventy-three."
I want to follow her blazing through the streets of
    Hokkaido
where she was born and grew up,
then to Texas, where her "beloved husband" died
and "without skipping a beat"
she entered the "food industry." What does this
mean? Where did she cook?
How many beats do we skip every day?

"In lieu of flowers," writes one of her sons,
"take your mother to dinner or enjoy a good meal
like Kazue would have wanted you to."

~

Yesterday we buried fiery Hilda, eighty-six, who
made everyone feel loved,
whose red poppies light up City Street each spring.
Did she call the whole world darling? No, just me,
just me.
But at her graveside, everyone else knew her better
than I did.
The neighborhood feels tipped.
Our house may slide into the river
without Hilda here, cozy in her tall rooms,
holding things back.

To Jamyla Bolden of Ferguson, Missouri

Fifty years before you did your homework
    in Ferguson
we did our homework in Ferguson, thinking life was
    fair.
If we didn't do our homework we might get a U—
    Unsatisfactory.
Your dad says you didn't even get to see the rest of
the world yet.
I've seen too much of the world and don't know
how to absorb this—a girl shot through a wall—
    U! U! U!
I'd give you some of my years if I could—
you should not have died that night—
there was absolutely no reason for you to die.
I'd like to be standing in a sprinkler with you,
the way we used to do, kids before air-conditioning,
safe with our friends in the drenching of cool,
safe with our shrieks, summer shorts, and happy hair.
Where can we go without thinking of you now?
Did you know there was a time Ferguson
was all a farm?

It fed St. Louis . . . giant meadows of corn,
sweet potatoes,
laden blackberry bushes, perfect tomatoes in crates,
and everything was shovels and hoes, and each life,
even the little tendril of a vine, mattered,
and you did your homework and got an S for
Satisfactory, Super,
instead of the S of Sorrow
now stamped on our hands.

Your Answering Machine,
After Your Death

Picks up after four rings
   And the hopeful lilt in your voice,
"I'll call you back as *soon* as I can,"
    gives no clue
           this will never happen

Under leaning gray-green trees
      doves stirring syllables at dawn
something unfinished
    ripples its long wave—
opera of air unfurling daily light
    shining on calendars

yours still
    pinned to the wall

Ring

A letter survives.
The stamp has been ripped from the envelope—
my grandfather Carl collected stamps.
This may have been one of the few letters
loitering in his sad last room
up north under towering trees.
Safe from cities and strangers—
unfortunately he was not safe
from the condescending words
of his teenaged granddaughter.
I wrote to him as if speaking to a dog.
Have you missed me? I'm sure you did not.
Sorry to be so silent but I have been traveling,
was on a happy horse ranch, at a conference
for global enlightenment, with my friends,
in my full delicious life.
He had written me a critical letter
about studying religion in college—
I wanted to set him straight.
The final paragraph blazes with
indignity—silly Grandpa, the world

cannot stay narrow anymore. We are
building bridges among religions, no one true path,
opening our minds . . . who was I?

Vivid youth, so full of myself
and my conviction, I could not bear
his smallness. Did he reply? My guess
would be no. But all these years
I have worn the last thing he gave me,
the only thing, a ring with one black stone.

Hummingbird

"The world is big and I want to have a good look at it before it gets dark."
                    —John Muir

Lyda Rose asked, "Are you a grown-up?"
The most flattering question of my adult life.
She darted around me like a hummingbird,
knotted in gauzy pink scarves,
braiding thyme into my hair.

There, on the brink of summer,
all summers blurred.
"No," I said.
"I don't think so.
I don't want to be."

"What are you then?"
Her dog snored by the couch,
little sister dozed on a pillow.
When her mom came home, we'd drink hot tea,
talk about our dead fathers, and cry.

"I think I'm a turtle," I said. "Hibernating."
"And a mouse in the moss.
And sometimes a hummingbird like you."

She jumped on my stomach then.
Asked if I'd ever worn a tutu
like the frayed pink one
she favored the whole spring.

No, not that.

"I have a shovel though," I said.
"For digging in the garden every night
before dark. And a small piano like yours
that pretends to be a harpsichord.
And I really love my broom."

~~~

Next Time Ask More Questions

Before leaping into something, remember
the span of time is long and gracious.
No one perches dangerously on any cliff
till you reply. Is there a pouch of rain
desperately thirsty people wait to drink from
if you say yes or no? I don't think so.
Never embrace "crucial" or "urgent"—
maybe for them?
Those are not your words.
Hold your horses and your mania and these
Hong Kong dollar coins in your pocket.
I'm not a corner or a critical turning page.
Wait. I'll think about it.
This pressure you share is a fantasy,
a misplaced hinge.
Maybe I'm already where I need to be.

In Transit

I mailed a package to myself, it never arrived.
Months later, wondering what it contained . . .
the package was oversized, I paid extra.
Mailed it from a place under trees. Surely shade
and sunlight was in the package. Mailed it
from a place compassionate to refugees.
Unopened envelopes inside the package,
poems from kind students hoping for response.
How do we answer without knowing
who they were or what they said?
This is why you must smile at everyone,
living and dead, everywhere you go.
You have no idea what has been lost
in transit.

Zen Boy

Why do you have
only one bowl?
I asked our son
helping him arrange
new kitchen cabinets
three plates
three mugs
three glasses
one bowl
a red oatmeal-
sized bowl
He smiled
I like
having only one bowl

Where Do Poets Find Images?

Giant stone turtle on a beach at Nansha, China.
Tired-looking father sits on the turtle,
gripping a child's striped jacket.
Toddlers scrabble in sand at his feet.
You will never be able to talk to him,
but can imagine something about him.
He lifts his eyes to you, but doesn't nod.

Or the tree with starry pink flowers
outside the classroom window.
Nobody knows its name, but the trunk has thorns,
everyone has a story involving the thorns.

It has always been this way—more nearby
than anyone could recall or describe.
M. C. Richards, who wrote *Centering*, said,
It takes a long time to learn that nothing is wasted.
She also said, Poets are not the only poets.

Here, a few glittering bits on a table.

What's on your table?

Tiny camel that travels thousands of miles

but still brays when you pinch its belly.

What can't you explain?

That motorized monkey with a scary face

pulling a child's rickshaw at the Fun Park.

Whose fun? The child looks terrified.

What surprised you lately?

Everything. Walking by water at sunset.

Remembering, I'm in China.

Evening ferry setting off for Hong Kong.

Cell Phone Tower Disguised as a Tree
Nansha, China

Spiky white tip at the top, the give-away.
Women kneel in gardens nearby, plucking weeds,
triangular straw hats on their heads,
rakes propped against real trees.
Do they feel a sizzling in the air?

Next to the tower, its false needles
a deeper piney green, real trees seem pale.
Invisible cobras burrow and slither
in the underbrush. "Be careful," kids say.
"They see you before you see them."

Guangdong Province,
"the most industrialized region on earth,"
gray skyscrapers pinned in line on horizons.
Everything IKEA sells is made here.
Easy to imagine the apartments' modestly sized
    interiors,
bathroom drains, steel sinks, kitchen stools,
bunks, modest light wood shelving, and the people

far from their home villages calling one another,
any way they can, between working hours,
from balconies, cupping weary hands over the phones,
calling through the tree.

Before I Was a Gazan

I was a boy
and my homework was missing,
paper with numbers on it,
stacked and lined,
I was looking for my piece of paper,
proud of this plus that, then multiplied,
not remembering if I had left it
on the table after showing to my uncle
or the shelf after combing my hair
but it was still somewhere
and I was going to find it and turn it in,
make my teacher happy,
make her say my name to the whole class,
before everything got subtracted
in a minute
even my uncle
even my teacher
even the best math student and his baby sister
who couldn't talk yet.
And now I would do anything
for a problem I could solve.

Morning Ablution

Such luxury—
we select a cup.
What power, politics?
We have a house.
Dry ground cracks
in multiple patterns.
Even if you can't fix everything
you can fix something.
I am allowed
to leave my country.
No one moves in
while I am gone.
What about moving in
while we are still here?
O Palestine!
If you plant something,
it might grow.

What Do Palestinians Want?

A man in the Lake District, England, asked me . . .

The pleasure of tending, tending
something that will not be taken away.
A family, a tree, growing for so long,
finally fruiting olives, the benevolence of branch,
and not to find a chopped trunk upon return.

Confidence in a threshold. A little green.
And quite a modest green untouched by drama.
Or a mound of calico coverlets stuffed with wool,
from one's own sheep, piled in a cupboard.
To find them still piled. Is that too much?

Not to dominate. Never to say we are the only
people who count,
or to be the only victims,
the chosen, more holy or precious.
No. Just to be ones who matter

as much as any other, in a common way, as you
might prefer.
Stones and books and daily freedom.
A little neighborly respect.

Arabs in Finland

Their language rolls out,
soft carpet in front of them.
They stroll beneath trees,
women in scarves,
men in white shirts,
belts, baggy trousers.
What they left to be here,
in the cold country,
where winter lasts forever,
haunts them in the dark—
golden hue of souk in sunlight,
gentle calling through streets that said,
Brother, Sister, sit with me a minute,
on the small stool
with the steaming glass of tea.
Sit with me.
We belong together.

Ladders in Repose

1

Glorious resting folded.

Humans with no desire for achievement beyond

apprehension of one clear moment after another

may appreciate you, not for what

you would help us do,

but—your neat rungs, calm radiance.

Against the side of the shed, all summer you shone.

I could have trimmed a tree.

Your silver song of waiting filled me.

2

Sometimes while driving far out among fields,

dry dead ruined fields, crisped by oil madness

and spill,

or the parched corn rows of August,

in the ditch by the road, a ladder.

You know it must have flown off a truck,

someone later missed it. Lying horizontal

among overgrown weeds, disappearing

nearly abandoned vertical dreams.

The Gift

Our neighbor Mrs. Esquivel
insists I haul her giant cactus away.
It's planted in a bucket.
Gives you thorns
when you barely brush past it.
Me no like it, please take, please help me,
she says again and again.
Me old. No good. Too big. It bites.
She's busy hanging four white socks
on her clothesline.
I return
with our green wheelbarrow.
The cactus tips over a lot
traveling to our house.
It's a cumbersome cactus.
Skin on fire. This cactus has a bad attitude.
Me no like it either but now
it's mine mine mine.

Voodoo Spoons

When her father the old man died
I was called to witness, to say
Yes, he really seems dead, and I knew
we were entering another phase.
No more would he raise his hand to me
from the porch across the park.
No more asking what I knew, begging for a hug,
thanking me for pie.
Now I had to hide from his daughter
whenever she came dragging a branch
or box down the sidewalk,
orange scarf tied under her chin.
The way she screamed my name
like a horror movie.
I had to dash inside
as if I hadn't heard, otherwise
doomed to many minutes of mad chat—
not one scrap of sense.
But I couldn't stop leaving things on her porch,
as I had done with her father for years . . .
it was my habit,

never guessing she would think
they came from a spirit on the other side,
a hawk, or a bat. Antique spoons in a bundle,
nubbly vintage suit with golden buttons,
holy card with glowing heart of wings.
He'd always known this meant, I'm thinking of you.
But she thought—they're watching,
I'm circled by eyes,
if I don't drink pomegranate juice, I'm doomed!

Barbershop

For Mary Endo, written about in the *Honolulu Star Advertiser*

Mary of Kalihi is closing down.

Today her last after sixty-two years of trimming hair,

soaping necks, Mary with the pink-and-white

candy-striped awning,

who gives an opinion, no topic taboo.

A man is quoted, "She was the one person

in my life I could always talk to."

Mary you could count on,

sixty-two years hardly a drop in the shaving mug,

bring her a thank you bigger than Honolulu,

bring her a hug, your whole life she was in here—

now banished by a landlord

you would personally like to shear.

What else will they build in this spot?

It's just a little shop.

Mary at ninety-one is taking it in stride.

She'll get dressed

next Monday as usual,

but "doesn't know where she'll go."

When you swing the door,

she's cutting a guy's hair
on her last day, wearing a ruffled pink apron,
her own hair perfectly styled.
She looks quizzical when you hand over
the newspaper feature
and one giant red rose.
Guy says, "See, Mary,
everybody loves you, even strangers!"
Four chairs of people waiting,
regulars lined up for a last conversation,
last clip. What is the size of this farewell?
Mary, Mary, you have such a strong grip.

Getaway Car, United States, 2017

Deep grooves of dust atop the books in our shelves.
Anyone else feel a constant need to apologize?
What happened in our nation? The only person
in our family who could translate is dead.

When I close my eyes, someone hopeful
cups a hand over a candle. This shadow has no face.
Weather, soon to deteriorate—I love how people
say that. Right now we find little refuge inside a
room.

Old Highway 90 heading west through Castroville . . .
a bakery offers square cheese pockets,
unsweet palm-sized delectable treats.
Maybe that's what we need.

Leaving the gray bulk of the city, ugly crush
of abandoned strip centers, sickening graffiti, happens
so quickly—a day's hand opens to release you.
Soon we will need to drive even farther,

to ruined towns like Langtry and Sanderson,
where the internet won't work to report
what our country has done. Maybe there is a cave
no one lived in since the Kiowa, with no writing
on any walls, no painted pictures of animals or
flames,
just an ancient heap of ashes in one corner.
There were times we thought the stone ages
behind us.

"Little Brother Shot Playing with Pistol"

His sister runs screaming from the church,
    jacket slips from one shoulder to the floor.
No carpet should be red today.

      No one singing, "Precious Lord."
For the next number, "I Won't Complain"
a crowd of wailing women rise up,
    aunties and grandmas banging handbags
    against the backs of pews.
"At least he's not suffering"—
      wouldn't most dead people
rather be suffering?

Moment of Relief

News loves to be bad.

It's a bad habit.

Think of all the good things people do—

Right now, how many people in our own town

are stirring soup to give away . . .

Bad news still gets more attention,

trash talk, insult . . .

At some point you make a decision.

Which world?

Malala, smiling warmly, speaks of dreams,

girls going to school,

mutual respect.

The newscasters stick her in

after lots of badness.

They know we can only take so much.

Unbelievable Things

1

My friend did not hear the sleek silent new electric
bus coming. She had stepped off a curb—the bus
threw her into the air. A woman with many children
dashed to her rescue. Although my friend was shaken
up and bruised, no bones were broken and she went
to work the next day. Within the same week, in an
entirely different part of town, my friend returned
to find her parked car had been hit, the side mirror
snapped off. A note of apology, with insurance
information, was folded under the windshield wiper.
The car had been hit by a bus.

2

I had lunch with the president of Finland while
wearing a gray linen shift dress I had purchased
for fifty cents in a thrift shop in Rock Springs,
Wyoming.

3

Michael pushed a shopping cart filled with boring
Home Depot items—wires, hoses, plumbing
connectives, a can of primer—toward his car. He
removed his hands from the cart for a moment to
reach into his pocket for keys and a man dashed up
from behind and began rolling the cart away. Hey,
wait a minute! Michael called out. What are you
doing?

The man said, Finders, Keepers.

4

Way up north in Aroostook County, Maine, the
town library was getting rid of books—massive heaps
of books lay scattered willy-nilly on long tables with
a sign—TAKE ANYTHING YOU WANT—FREE.
Why? I asked the librarian. What is wrong with these
books? I stared at the library shelves. They weren't
stuffed. We don't want them, the librarian said. They
are of no use to us anymore. Does that mean no
one checked them out for a while? She shrugged,
exhibiting no remorse. But a great sadness swept
over me and I began browsing. Hardbacks mostly—

biographies, Adlai Stevenson and Gandhi, novels, short stories, expeditions—mostly early- and mid-twentieth century editions. Some had engraved-style covers and were even older. I thought of my brother-in-law in New Zealand who collects and sells books about adventure and I hiked straight down to the Dollar Store to buy the most heavy-duty black trash bags available. Good thing I'd been assigned to work in that town for a whole week.

Every day I visited the library and packed a bag with books, then hauled it up the hill to where I was staying. I asked my hosts if I might leave the books in the front hallway so I didn't have to lug them all up the stairs—my room was in the attic. They stared at me dubiously. I urged them to get down to the library.

At the middle school where I was working, I pressed the writing students. Hey people, you *must* get over to the library. Do it today. Great books are sitting there free waiting for you to claim them. You won't even have to return them.

They stared at me. I never saw a single student at the library.

On Friday after school, I arrived to find the long tables gone. The librarian pointed to the back door when she saw me. They're outside now, she said.

A mountain of lovely books lay on the ground behind the library, recklessly pitched.

I felt dizzy, sick. Marched back inside.

What happens to them next?

They go to the town dump.

My brain was whirling. Was there a criminal code for this?

The next day my husband would return from his own work in Canada to collect me and drive home to Texas. He would be shocked to see how my baggage had grown.

One of the books I took home with me was about a 1920s man who walked alone across Africa, something my bookseller brother-in-law had also done. This would be a perfect present for him. Later I heard he sold that book, that slightly tattered book with the empty library card pocket still inside its cover (which they say reduces the value), for $500.

5

I mailed a letter to my friend Howard Peacock, who
liked to strut by the river between our dwellings,
staring into water, meditating on turtles and cranes.
Howard had a long white beard and a deeply
southern, elegant way of speaking. He rented a
small apartment in the Granada, an old downtown
building which used to be a hotel. Howard gave me
his dead wife's casserole cookbook, which I never
used because it was mostly meat. But I wanted to
thank him, so mailed him a letter. I could just have
walked down to the river and handed it to him. I
also thanked him for saving the Big Thicket in east
Texas which everyone said he and his late wife had
fairly singlehandedly preserved, throwing themselves
down in front of bulldozers, and a good thing,
because those forests are profound and precious like
all great things people struggle to preserve. He never
mentioned my letter till five years had passed and he
called. Did you write me a letter five years ago?
Uh, I think so. Maybe. Why? I got it today. Nearly
five years to the day since you wrote it. Seriously. I'm
mailing the envelope back to you right now as proof.

It had taken my letter five years to travel six blocks.
I carried the envelope with both our addresses on it
to the post office and asked the clerk, Do you have
any idea where this letter might have been for five
whole years? The clerk gazed at me with his deep sad
eyes and said, Nope. It could have been anywhere.

6

Your parents met each other. Anybody met anybody.
Out of all the possible people who might have been
born, you were born.
Constant miracles. But who remembers them?
Before the great film critic Roger Ebert died, he said,
I believe I was perfectly all right before I was born
and I think I'll be fine later too.
We walk around the block, stride up the hillside. Is
it this year or last? Something strange is happening.
We're so anxious but deep down, in the heart place
of time, our lives are resonant, rolling. They're just

waiting for us to remember them. They are very patient and quiet. We are here, so deeply here, and then we won't be.

And it is the most unbelievable thing of all.

Airport Life

1

Loudspeaker announcement (San Antonio, Texas)

Attention in the terminal!

Would the passenger   who left a bucket of stones

      with a candle stuck in them

          please

    return to   the security

        checkpoint?

My shock—sitting at A3—I am the only one
laughing.

Businessmen aren't laughing.

They didn't even hear it.

Repeat announcement . . .

Everyone looks bored. They are checking their
phones.

They are telling people where they are.

2

Man on cell phone (Jeddah, Saudi Arabia)

Good-bye! Bye-bye, my sweethearts!

    Love you!

        Send email! Send pictures! Don't forget!

          Pray, do everything!!!!!

And take care!

~~⧓~~

Texas, Out Driving

The Solid Rock Church of Kerrville
has moved to another location.
It says so on the sign under the name—Solid Rock.
Also the entire town of Comfort
appears to be for sale.
This does not feel comforting at all.
How many times we drove these curves,
pale fence posts, bent cedars . . .
but nothing needs us here.
Nothing we said, thought, forgot,
took root in the ditch around the bend.
I always want to stop at historic markers,
see what happened long before, but
the pull of motion keeps a car going,
passing by till next time,
which soon won't come,
even when everything we know
says *slow.*

Missing the Boat, Take Two

We sat on a long wooden pier,
waiting for a boat for one full hour.
Stared at gentle wavelets,
chatted with a sailor,
read about Maine,
reminisced.
Then the boat sneaked in so quietly,
pulled up at a slant behind our backs,
loaded passengers,
we never turned our heads into the sun to see,
the boat slipped away from the dock,
we were shocked.

I hope dying could feel like this.

All We Will Not Know

For Adriana Corral

Before dawn, trembling in air down to the old river,
circulating gently as a new season
delicate yet in its softness, rustling raiment
of hopes never stitched tightly enough to any hour.
I was almost, maybe, just about, going to do that.
A girl's thick hair, brushed over one shoulder
so often no one could imagine it not being there.
Hair as a monument. Voice as a monument.
Hovering—pitched.
Beloved sister, maker of plans, main branch,
we need you desperately, where have you gone?
Here is the sentence called No no no no no.
Come back, everything grants you your freedom,
Here in the mire of too much thinking,
we drown, we drown, split by your echo.

Loving Working

"We clean to give space for Art."
—Micaela Miranda, Freedom Theatre, Palestine

Work was a shining refuge when wind sank its tooth
into my mind. Everything you love is going away,
drifting, but you could sweep this stretch of floor,
this patio or porch, gather white stones in a bucket,
rake the patch for future planting, mop the counter
with a rag. Lovely wet gray rag, squeeze it hard,
it does so much. Clear the yard of blowing bits of
    plastic.
The glory in the doing. Breath of the doing.
Sometimes the simplest move kept fear from
fragmenting into no energy at all, or sorrow from
multiplying, or sorrow from being the only person
living in the house.

Stars Over Big Bend

Maybe we first met this arching dome
in dreams of what a life could be.
Sheer spaciousness, before hope
bent backward too many times,
breaking news breaking us.
In the vast immensity
a breath feels more at home,
released into place.
Never mind which star might be dead,
how long ago it died—
don't want to know.
Light taking forever to get here,
more precious when it arrives.
Far-ranging, brilliance to quietude,
legacies of patience, belonging, disappearing.
And if the stars do not remember us, they act
otherwise.

United

When sleepless, it's helpful to meditate
on mottoes of the states.
South Carolina, "While I breathe I hope."
Perhaps this could be
the new flag on the empty flagpole.
Or "I Direct" from Maine—
Why, because Maine gets the first sunrise?
How bossy, Maine!
In Arkansas, "The People Rule." Lucky you.
Kansas, "To the Stars Through Difficulties"—
clackety wagon wheels, long land
and the droning press of heat—cool stars, relief.
Idaho, "Let it be perpetual"—now this is strange.
Idaho, what is your "it"?
Who chose these lines?
How many contenders?
What would my motto be tonight, in tangled sheets?
Texas, "Friendship"—now boasts the Open Carry
    law.
Wisconsin, where my mother's parents are buried,
chose "Forward." Washington, wisest, "By and By."

New Mexico, "It Grows as It Goes"—
now this is scary.
Two dangling "*it*s." This does not represent
that glorious place.
West Virginia, "Mountaineers are always free"—
really?
Oklahoma must be tired, "Labor conquers all things."
Oklahoma, get together with Nevada, who chose
only "Industry" as motto.
I think of Nevada as a playground,
or mostly empty. How wrong we are
about one another.
For Alaska to pick "North to the Future"
seems odd. Where else are they going?

Reserved for Poets

(Signs on first rows of chairs at poetry festival, La Conner,
Washington)

Sunsets.

Trouble.

Full moons.

No really—they're everybody's.

Nothing is reserved.

We're all poets rippling with

layers of memories,

mostly what we might forget.

Let it belong. Every pocket,

satchel, hand.

We forgot to make a reservation.

But there's room.

Her Father Still Watching

For Doris Duke, whose father's last words were said to have been "Trust no one"

You can trust me, said white marble

Trust us more, said black volcanic rocks

The palm tree said, I deserve nothing but trust

And the clouds drifting swiftly
said nothing but held
their trust sacred

Small Basket of Happiness

It would never call your name.
But it would be waiting somewhere close,
perhaps under a crushed leaf
turned from pale green to gold
with no fanfare.
You hadn't noticed
the gathered hush
of a season's tipping.
Shadows flowing past
before any light came up,
people whom only a few
might remember,
so much accompaniment
inside a single breeze.
All whom we loved.
In the quiet air lived
the happiness they had given.
And would still give, if only.
You would slow down a minute.
You would bend.

Biographical Notes

Here are a few biographical notes on the great voices mentioned in this book that have inspired and encouraged me and so many others over the years.

Read on, friends, read on! We have never read or listened enough.

Galway Kinnell—Lived in New York and Vermont. Kinnell used to say we need to taste poems in our mouths, roll them over and over to appreciate them. Don't miss his *When One Has Lived a Long Time Alone* or *A New Selected Poems*, which reads like a feast. (Introduction)

Abraham Lincoln—Sixteenth American president, whom we miss very much. He didn't write any books (although so many have been written about him), but we hear his voice in his speeches and should probably all read "The Gettysburg Address" on a regular basis. (Introduction)

William Stafford—Born in Kansas, taught in Oregon, traveled widely, conscientious objector, one of the most essential voices of the twentieth century. *The Way It Is*, published after his death, brings together many of his most indelible poems. His *Every War Has Two Losers*, edited by his son Kim after his death, should be chained to a pedestal in the Oval Office. (Introduction and "Woven by Air, Texture of Air" and "Tell Us All the Gossip You Know")

Peter Matthiessen—Prolific American writer, environmentalist, and activist. Lived on Long Island and loved birding. So many people say their lives have been changed by *The Snow Leopard*. He preferred his fiction to his nonfiction, though. (Introduction and "Warbler Woods")

Juna Hewitt—Young artist/student from Yokohama, Japan, and New York. (Introduction)

Freya Stark—British author who lived 100 years and wrote about travel (especially Middle Eastern) and culture. Her book *The Journey's Echo* (first American edition in 1964), with sections written in the '30s, '40s, and '50s, is particularly haunting to read in the twenty-first century. (Introduction)

Townes Van Zandt—Great singer/songwriter from a historic Texas family, whose most well-known song was "Pancho and Lefty." But "If I Needed You" and so many other beautiful songs he wrote will never disappear. (Introduction)

Hallie Stillwell—Rancher, historian, lived in Big Bend National Park, Texas, and wrote *How Come It's Called That? Place Names in the Big Bend Country.* ("Big Bend National Park Says No to All Walls")

Ralph Karam—Lebanese-Texan who started a classic Mexican restaurant on Zarzamora Street in San Antonio—restaurant now demolished. ("Little Lady, Little Nugget Brooms")

Henry David Thoreau—Transcendentalist, friend of Ralph Waldo Emerson, author of the inestimable *Walden Pond*, lived a short but deep life in Concord, Massachusetts. My friend Joe Coomer owns a pencil made by Henry's family's company. Thoreau wrote, "The wind that blows is all that anybody knows." ("Lost People")

Aziz Shihab—My father, born in Jerusalem in 1927. Journalist, author of *Does the Land Remember Me? A Memoir of Palestine*, activist, and public speaker. ("For Aziz," "Getting Over It," "Every Day," "Double Peace")

Rosa Bonheur—French artist of nineteenth century, especially loved painting animals. She was disruptive in traditional schools. ("*Sheep by the Sea*, a painting by Rosa Bonheur (1865)")

Emily Dickinson—One of the most famously beloved, mysteriously reclusive, and succinct American poets there ever will be. A recent compelling volume of her 52 "envelope poems"—written on flaps and fragments—is called *The Gorgeous Nothings*. ("Emily" and "Tell Us All the Gossip You Know")

Maya Angelou—Writer of poems, memoirs, also a civil rights activist, dancer, actor, public speaker of tremendous power. Her birth name was Marguerite Annie Johnson. Her second volume of essays is called *Even the Stars Look Lonesome*. ("Gratitude Pillow")

John Masefield—British poet who also once worked in a carpet factory in the U.S. Obsessed from childhood with reading; one of his own books was called *The Box of Delights*. ("Life Loves")

Elizabeth Barrett Browning—Great British poet, oldest of twelve children, married Robert Browning. *Sonnets from the Portuguese* contains 44 love sonnets—Number 43 begins with the classic lines, "How do I love thee? Let me count the ways." ("Life Loves")

Coleman Barks—Poet, renowned translator, and presenter of Rumi poems; resident of Athens, Georgia. Do not miss his own poems in *Hummingbird Sleep*. ("Getting Over It")

Susan Gilbert Harvey—Artist and writer from Rome, Georgia. *Tea with Sister Anna: A Personal History* is a personal history/magical travel book in one delicious read. ("Getting Over It")

Grace Paley—Political activist, writer, and teacher. Powerfully outspoken, was a tomboy as a child. *The Little Disturbances of Man* is one of her classics, humorous and haunting. ("Conversation with Grace Paley, Flight of the Mind Writing Workshop, Oregon")

Lucille Clifton—Poet and widely beloved professor of poetry. Some of her early poems were published in an anthology edited by Langston Hughes. Her later *Blessing the Boats* is a great companion to keep nearby. ("Showing Up")

Caroline Mueller—She and her husband Al operated Mueller Organic Farm (founded 1883), producing lush organic crops in Ferguson, Missouri. She got her first library card in her eighties—had procrastinated all those years, thinking they cost money. ("For Caroline M." and Al appears in "What Happens Next")

José Emilio Pacheco—One of Mexico's foremost poets and writers of prose, also a literary critic, died at age 74. His book *El silencio de la luna* (*The Silence of the Moon*) won the Premio Jose Asuncion Silva for the best book in Spanish in any country between 1990–95. ("Tomorrow")

Paul Durcan—Irish poet, resident of Dublin. Do not miss *A Snail in My Prime*. ("After Listening to Paul Durcan, Ireland")

Leo Kottke—Genius acoustic guitarist and singer. Plays both 6- and 12-string guitars. ("We Will Get Lost in You")

Joni Mitchell—Prolific Canadian singer/songwriter whose album *Blue* is one of the most beloved and widely memorized albums of all time. ("We Will Get Lost in You")

Tish Hinojosa—Latina singer born near the river in San Antonio, has also lived in Austin and Germany, sings in both Spanish and English. *After the Fair* is one of her many stunning albums. ("We Will Get Lost in You")

Bruce Springsteen—Legendary New Jersey singer/songwriter whose memoir *Born to Run* is simply exquisite. ("We Will Get Lost in You")

Robert Johnson—Renowned blues singer who recorded his songs in the Gunter Hotel, San Antonio, Texas. Died mysteriously at twenty-seven. Try his "Walkin' Blues" when you need some blues. ("We Will Get Lost in You")

Patty Griffin—Mesmerizing singer/songwriter originally from Maine. You just can't get much better than *Living with Ghosts* or *1000 Kisses* or *Children Running Through*. ("We Will Get Lost in You")

Joanna Newsom—Amazing harpist & singer. *Divers* is a good place to begin. ("We Will Get Lost in You")

Sara Thomsen—Singer/songwriter, founder of Echoes of Peace Choir, and chicken-raiser living near Duluth, Minnesota. You also can't get much better than *Winter Wanderings, Somewhere to Begin*, or *Everything Changes*. ("We Will Get Lost in You")

James Tate—Elegant, humorous American poet who lived and taught in Amherst, also collected quilts. *Distance from Loved Ones* is an amazing book. ("James Tate in Jerusalem")

Langston Hughes—African American poet, novelist, activist, leader of the Harlem Renaissance though originally from the American Midwest. *The Big Sea* is his fascinating autobiography. ("Train Across Texas" and mentioned in "What Happens Next")

Henry Wadsworth Longfellow—Classic American poet who lived in Cambridge, Massachusetts, and had six children. His house museum is one of the best literary sites in the nation. Many people grew up reading *Evangeline* and *The Song of Hiawatha*. ("Longfellow's Bed")

Walt Whitman—Often called the "Father of Modern American Poetry." His *Leaves of Grass* has appeared in countless editions—the White House once displayed a compact first edition in a glass case. ("Walt Whitman's Revisions" and "Tell Us All the Gossip You Know")

Jack Kerouac—Deeply compelling favorite writer of millions of readers; novelist best known for *On the Road*, but many found *The Dharma Bums* a better book. He believed in spontaneous prose for a good part of his writing life. ("Rest and Be Kind, You Don't Have to Prove Anything" and "Tell Us All the Gossip You Know")

Stella Kerouac—Last wife of Jack Kerouac, Greek heritage, originally from Lowell, Massachusetts. She wrote good handwritten letters. ("Rest and Be Kind, You Don't Have to Prove Anything")

Allen Ginsberg—American poet often considered one of founders of the Beat Generation, highly anti-militaristic and anti-materialistic. His *Howl* broke the world wide open. ("Rest and Be Kind, You Don't Have to Prove Anything")

Peace Pilgrim—Mysterious wanderer and lecturer about world peace and inner peace who would not give her real age or name while she walked on her endless speaking tour thousands of miles across the country. She never wrote a book, but after her death (oddly in a car accident, though for many years she would barely get in a car) her friends compiled some of her talks in a book anyone may obtain free online from the Friends of Peace Pilgrim website (www.peacepilgrim.org). We need it. ("Peace Pilgrim's Pocket")

C. D. Wright—American poet originally from Arkansas; Chancellor of the Academy of American Poets at the time of her death. Do not miss her roundly celebrated and profoundly original *One With Others*. ("C. D. Stepped Out")

Robert Louis Stevenson—Scottish writer whose poems were precious parts of many childhoods worldwide and whose novels quickly became classics. *A Child's Garden of Verses* has been in my custody since I was six—gripped tightly, same edition. ("True Success")

Robert Bly—American poet from Minnesota who founded the "Great Mother" summer poetry camps. A legendary energetic guide; his *Silence in the Snowy Fields* opened up new, crisp worlds for so many poetry readers. ("Tell Us All the Gossip You Know")

Leonard Nathan—American poet, critic, and professor of rhetoric at UC Berkeley. See his *Dear Blood*, which makes every moment feel more dear. ("Tell Us All the Gossip You Know")

Mary Oliver—American poet whose contemplative, resonant work is deeply influenced by the natural world. Try *New & Selected Poems* or *Why I Wake Early*. ("Tell Us All the Gossip You Know")

Ernest Hemingway—American writer who lived many places, including Cuba and Idaho. *A Moveable Feast* is a favorite. ("Tell Us All the Gossip You Know")

Ruth Stone—Wondrous poet and teacher, originally from Virginia, later of Vermont. *Second-Hand Coat* is brilliant. ("Tell Us All the Gossip You Know")

Josephine Miles—Poet and Professor at UC Berkeley for many years. Go with *To All Appearances: Poems New and Selected*. ("Tell Us All the Gossip You Know")

Genine Lentine—Writer, educator, passionate gardener living in San Francisco. See *The Wild Braid: A Poet Reflects on a Century in the Garden*, which she made with centenarian poet Stanley Kunitz when she worked as his literary assistant in the last years of his life. ("Tell Us All the Gossip You Know")

William Burroughs—Writer, painter, performer, who was open about his use of drugs. *Naked Lunch*, his novel from

1959, contained small stories he said could be read in any order. ("Tell Us All the Gossip You Know")

Ken Kesey—Writer, countercultural figure, wrote *One Flew Over the Cuckoo's Nest*, which became a movie, and many other books. He said, "I was too young to be a beatnik and too old to be a hippie." ("Tell Us All the Gossip You Know")

William Goyen—Writer of short stories and novels who grew up in southeast Texas but lived in New York and Los Angeles. *House of Breath* is a classic book of stories. ("Tell Us All the Gossip You Know")

Mark Twain—American writer and humorist whose real name was Samuel Clemens. He signed at least one book with "Be good and you will be lonesome." I held it in my own hands. It's rather astonishing that he insisted his massive three-volume *Autobiography of Mark Twain* not be published till one hundred years after his death. Has anyone else ever done that? ("Tell Us All the Gossip You Know")

Thomas Edison—Hello, lightbulbs! Edison did not write books, but self-published a newspaper at age fourteen and wrote many papers now archived at Rutgers University. Quite a few other people have written books about him. ("Tell Us All the Gossip You Know")

Daria Donnelly—Brilliant educator and writer on children's literature for *Commonweal*; lived in Cambridge, Massachusetts. ("Tell Us All the Gossip You Know")

Garth Williams—Illustrator of classic children's books, including *Charlotte's Web* and *Stuart Little*. He once ate dinner at our table. We were spellbound. ("Tell Us All the Gossip You Know")

John Steinbeck—American writer whose book *The Grapes of Wrath* won the Pulitzer Prize. ("Tell Us All the Gossip You Know")

Edward Said—Palestinian scholar, professor, and writer who taught for many years at Columbia University. His *Out of Place: A Memoir* is a classic of literature of exile. Possibly the smartest person I ever met. ("One State")

Chief Joseph—Succeeded his father as leader of the Nez Percé tribe, who were indigenous to the Wallowa Valley in Oregon and then cast out. His famous and brief "I will Fight No More Forever" speech should be read regularly by all people. ("My Name Is . . .")

Yehuda Amichai—Israeli poet, born in Germany, who lived in Jerusalem and was considered Israel's greatest modern poet. Get *The Selected Poetry of Yehuda Amichai*. ("Double Peace")

Samih al-Qasim—Palestinian journalist and poet, crucial "resistance voice" of Israel's Arab community. ("Break the Worry Cocoon")

Vera B. Williams—Beloved American artist and writer of children's books, including *A Chair for My Mother.* ("Please Sit Down")

Dorothy Stafford—Oregon hero, mother of four, friend of thousands, educator, was married to poet William Stafford. She collected magical sayings of her children when they were small and made beautiful limited-edition books. ("For the Birds")

John O'Donahue—Beloved Irish writer and contemplative speaker who wrote many books including *Anam Cara.* "When you cease to fear your solitude, a new creativity awakens in you." ("Bowing Candles")

Van Morrison—Brilliant international music icon for more than 50 years; from Belfast, Northern Ireland. One favorite song: "When Heart is Open" from his *Common One* album. ("Black Car")

Frankee Liddy—Resident of Belfast, Northern Ireland. He writes, "I realized I had only 1 life. This is it." ("Belfast")

Ryushin Paul Haller—Zen Teacher and former longtime co-abbot at the San Francisco Zen Center. His *Dharma Talks,* which one may listen to free online, are immense gifts of spirit and wisdom. ("Belfast")

Jamyla Bolden—Child of Ferguson, Missouri, life cut short by random bullet. ("To Jamyla Bolden of Ferguson, Missouri")

Carl Allwardt—My maternal grandfather, devout Lutheran, who lived for decades on Union Boulevard in St. Louis. ("Ring")

John Muir—Born in Scotland, founder of the Sierra Club, hero of American hiking trails, forests, natural preserves, wilderness; don't miss *My First Summer in the Sierra*. ("Hummingbird")

Lyda Rose Martin—Daughter of poet Jenny Browne and photographer Scott Martin. ("Hummingbird")

M. C. Richards—Educator, creator of pottery and poems, was part of the first "happening" with John Cage; her book *Centering in Pottery, Poetry, and the Person* was a life-changer. ("Where Do Poets Find Images?")

Mary Endo—Cut hair in same shop in Honolulu for a really long time. Some of her customers said she was the one person in their lives they could always talk to without shame. ("Barbershop")

Malala Yousafzai—Youngest person ever to win Nobel Peace Prize; Pakistani activist for justice and female education.

Valiantly survived assassination attempt. ("Moment of Relief")

Michael Nye—My photographer/documentarian husband—see www.michaelnye.org; forthcoming—his first book from Trinity University Press. ("Unbelievable Things")

Howard Peacock—Was a lifelong eco-activist and writer who helped create the Big Thicket National Preserve in east Texas—battled many big lumber companies in the process. ("Unbelievable Things")

Roger Ebert—Famous film critic who lived in Chicago; see *Life Itself*, a 2014 documentary about his life. ("Unbelievable Things")

Adriana Corral—Artist of haunting installations, performances, and sculptures, San Antonio, Texas. ("All We Will Not Know")

Micaela Miranda—Director at the Freedom Theatre, a community theater and cultural project in Jenin Refugee Camp, Palestine—"Resistance through Art." ("Loving Working")

Doris Duke—Heir to great fortune, envisioned Shangri La (Honolulu) when she was 22, worked on it all her life. Collector, philanthropist. ("Her Father Still Watching")

Index of First Lines

I had not noticed 37
I mailed a package to myself, it never arrived. 132
I pledge allegiance 113
I was a boy 138
I'd like to take Donald Trump to Palestine, 111
I'm attached to everything 118
If this is the best you can do, citizens of the world, 27
In 1972 I sat with Stella Kerouac in her St. 70
In icy fields. 28
Is it possible to fall in love posthumously with 122
It's been a spectacular day, Grace! 50
It would never call your name. 171

Jesse never felt smarter than at age six 109
Joni Mitchell said in an interview, Everything I am, 61

Langston, what did Texas look like back then, 65
Lyda Rose asked, "Are you a grown-up?" 129

Mary of Kalihi is closing down. 147
May polar bears welcome you 15
Maya loved the jingle of the massive key ring 43
Maybe we first met this arching dome 166
My friend did not hear the sleek silent new electric 153

Never too proud to tip his head back. 41
News loves to be bad. 152
Not for him and his people alone 94

One boy in our grade school was considered 9
Our neighbor Mrs. Esquivel 144

Picks up after four rings 126
Popping profusely   small shoots of glimmering 12
Poured full of ripe language 59

seems too short for a man, especially one with 67
She wanted to be a window wherever she walked. 11
She writes to me— 1
Some birds hide in leaves so effectively 80

Acknowledgments

Poetry Magazine; *Texas Monthly Magazine*; *Rusted Radishes* (Beirut); *Massachusetts Review*; *World Poetry Portfolio* (India); *Mizna*; *Washington Square Review*; *Happiness, The Delight-Tree: An Anthology of Contemporary International Poetry*, edited by Bhikshuni Weisbrot, Darrel Alejandro Holmes, and Elizabeth Lara; *Poet Lore*; *No Tokens*; *The San Antonio Express-News*; *San Pedro River Review*; *The Café Review*; Pomelo Books; *The Progressive*; *Plough Quarterly*; *The MacGuffin*

"Big Bend National Park Says No to All Walls," "Songbook," "Next Time Ask More Questions," "To Jamyla Bolden of Ferguson, Missouri," and "The Tent" originally appeared on Poets.org. Reprinted by permission of the Academy of American Poets, 75 Maiden Lane, Suite 901, New York, NY 10038. www.poets.org.

"Her Father Still Watching" reprinted by permission of Shangri La, Doris Duke Foundation for Islamic Art. From unpublished chapbook, *Dear Doris*.

Thanks to U2/Bono for streaming "United" on the 2017 Joshua Tree tour.

Thanks to Shangri La, Doris Duke Foundation for Islamic Art, Honolulu, Hawai'i, for the best month of our lives.